ADVANCE PRAISE FOR
SECURITY FOR HOLY PLACES

Dr. Stephen Bryen is a Renaissance man in matters of strategy and military technology. In this new book he again shows his deep knowledge of the issues, exhaustive knowledge of sources and sensitivity to the human factor in tactical situations. It is a must-read for anyone concerned with countering terror against holy places.

P. Goldman, Wax Family Fellow at the ιst Forum, Senior Fellow at the London or Policy Research, and member of the of Advisers of Sino-Israel Government Network and Academic Leadership

Security for Holy Places is the book I have been looking for over two years. The book is impressive with its level of depth and background and gives excellent advice on how to proceed to make one's congregation a safer place. It is well organized and most helpful. I recommend that every leader of holy congregations read this book, take it to heart, and put it into practice.

--M.A. Golden, Security Technology Expert, Columbus Ohio

This book by Stephen Bryen is a great book to read and a very useful guide for clergy and security experts or even lay persons who are concerned about security in holy places and areas of worship. Violent attacks and intrusions against holy places have increased and are growing. Stephen's style of writing is very clear and easy to follow. I have recommended the book to many of the local religious establishments here in London and I certainly recommend it strongly to all those concerned about improving security arrangements in these establishments.

--Dr. Goran Talabani, Former Senior Lecturer at Imperial College School of Medicine, London, UK

Steve Bryen's newest book, Security for Holy Places, *is a timely, insightful and informative read. Understanding the threats and identifying vulnerable situations is a must in today's world. Lay leadership needs to be in intimately involved in this process. Prayer alone will not protect sacred places in 2019 and beyond. I strongly endorse Steve's work.*

--Tom Malatesta, Blue Taurus Partnership, Chicago

Steve Bryen is one of our nation's most respected national security experts. Now he turns his sights to a problem close to home, the security of churches, synagogues, and mosques. After so many mass shootings, protecting our holy places has become increasingly frustrating for community leaders, who have been taught by the FBI to be passive recipients of potential threat information, and then to follow their model of "Run, Hide, Fight."

Dr. Bryen examines a broad array of mass shootings and draws sober conclusions that stray from the hand-wringing and political correctness you hear so often on TV. Gun laws "do not really do much to protect citizens from gun violence," he notes. And relying on local law enforcement to provide early warning of individual threats is a mistake, since many active shooters have never been on the radar of law enforcement.

Instead, he proposes a new operational model for dealing with potential and actual threats that focuses on hardening physical security, training security personnel to intercept and isolate an active shooter, while protecting as many people as possible from harm.

In the dozens of examples he explores in this timely book, Dr. Bryen shows how his new security model can save lives—and prevent many attacks from happening in the first place.

--Kenneth R. Timmerman, Security Journalist & Author

Given the increasing numbers of armed attacks on US religious groups it is imperative for religious leaders to develop plans to meet these threats.

Dr. Bryen's book, Security for Holy Places, *is replete with examples of actual security breaches and how his recommended security planning solutions could have stopped or mitigated loss of life.*

Congregation leaders who have yet to act must now "plan the plan" and implement their plan with the minimum essential resources necessary to protect their members.

Dr. Bryen has been engaged in a lifetime of national and international physical and technological security policy planning to inform this timely security contribution. I encourage congregation leaders and members to read this book, then create and implement their unique plan today.

--Howard Ady, Defense Corporate Executive
and Episcopalian, Carlsbad, California

Dr. Stephen Bryen has provided an invaluable service to synagogues and house of worship around the world. He brings enormous expertise and brilliance to this incredibly important subject. I highly recommend that all congregations make use of his recommendations.

--Rabbi Shmuel Herzfeld, Rabbi *at* Ohev Sholom,
The National Synagogue, Washington DC

Security for Holy Places

SECURITY
FOR
HOLY PLACES

HOW TO BUILD A SECURITY PLAN FOR YOUR
CHURCH, SYNAGOGE, MOSQUE, OR TEMPLE

STEPHEN BRYEN

NASHVILLE

NEW YORK • LONDON • MELBOURNE • VANCOUVER

Security for Holy Places

How to Build a Security Plan for Your Church, Synagoge, Mosque, or Temple

© 2020 Stephen D. Bryen

Published in New York, New York, by Morgan James Publishing. Morgan James is a trademark of Morgan James, LLC. www.MorganJamesPublishing.com

ISBN 9781642798517 paperback
ISBN 9781642798524 eBook
Library of Congress Control Number: 2019951700

Cover Design Concept: Rob Williams

Cover Design and Interior Design by:
Chris Treccani
www.3dogcreative.net

Morgan James is a proud partner of Habitat for Humanity Peninsula and Greater Williamsburg. Partners in building since 2006.

Get involved today! Visit
MorganJamesPublishing.com/giving-back

DISCLAIMER

The information contained on this book is for general information purposes only. Neither the author nor SDB Partners LLC assumes any responsibility for errors or omissions in the book.

This book is designed to provide information and motivation to our readers. It is provided as a public service with the understanding that the author and copyright holder is not engaged to render any type of professional advice. The content of each chapter is the sole expression and opinion of its author. No warranties or guarantees are expressed or implied. Neither the publisher nor the individual author shall be liable for any physical, psychological, emotional, financial, or commercial damages, including, but not limited to, special, incidental, consequential or other damages. Our views and rights are the same: You are responsible for your own choices, actions, and results.

The author reserves the right to make additions, deletions, or modification to the contents of the book at any time without prior notice.

The book may contain references to external websites that are not provided or maintained by or in any way affiliated with the author. Please note that the author does not guarantee the accuracy, relevance, timeliness, or completeness of any information contained herein.

This book does not endorse any products and any surmise that it does so is incorrect.

The author has no connection to any product company, vendor or distributor, mentioned in the book.

This book is designed for educational purposes only. You should not rely on this information as a substitute for, nor does it replace, professional security advice or recommendations and support by vendors.

To the volunteers who help our holy places stay safe and to the guards and police who defend them

Nehemiah 4:9
But we prayed to our God, and because of them we set up a guard against them day and night

Surah Al-Hijr, 46
"Enter ye here in peace and security"

A SHOUT OUT TO HEROES

Officer Timothy Matson is one of the police heroes who fought to subdue and capture the active shooter at the Tree of Life Synagogue in Pittsburgh, Pennsylvania.

Officer Matson suffered eleven gunshot wounds. Taken to the hospital after the shooter was captured, he was listed in critical condition. He required many surgeries, and still has one pending. He spent nearly four months in the hospital.

Another SWAT team member, Officer Anthony Burke, who was with Matson was shot in the hand

Officer Timothy Matson (Cashman Photos, courtesy of RJC)

Officer Michael Smidga was wounded by shrapnel that hit his face.

Two other officers, John Persin and Tyler Pashel, suffered minor injuries.

What Officer Matson and his fellow police officers did was courageous but not extraordinary. Law enforcement and First Responder personnel deserve not only our praise but our support.

TABLE OF CONTENTS

FOREWORD

By Rabbi Arnold E. Resnicoff*

Reading *Security for Holy Places* brought back a flood of memories:

From my early training in the Navy, when we "war-gamed" what to do in case of danger, and that included being on an airplane during an attempted skyjacking. We were to try to hide our military IDs if possible, and then cooperate with the skyjacker. Of course, after 9-11, when we realized planes might not simply be diverted—but instead, used as weapons—our thinking changed dramatically.

From my knowledge of Jewish history, when Jews would often pray in secret to avoid attacks—or sometimes have secret exits in synagogues to use in case of danger. Today's Touro Synagogue in Newport, RI, still has a trap door, although tour guides explain that it is symbolic, to remind worshippers to celebrate their freedom today, as opposed to the time their Spanish-Portuguese ancestors feared dangers like the Inquisition.

From my time in the rivers of Vietnam's Mekong Delta, when we fired at branches floating toward us in the river...just in case the branch was camouflage to hide an enemy Viet Cong swimmer who was carrying explosives.

From my own family stories about my great-grandfather Solomon Greenberg, who was mortally wounded by stone-throwing gang members under the Brooklyn Bridge, because they identified him as a Jew—and saw him as an "easy target."

From my experience in Beirut October 23, 1983, the day of the Beirut Barracks bombing, when a terrorist drove a bomb-filled truck into one of our two barracks buildings, killing 241 American military personnel: 220 from the Marines, 3 from the Army, and 18 from the Navy.

Many of my memories, and much of my training, has shaped my life – and makes me appreciate the need for this book.

From left: Major General Fiume Gqiba, Chief of Chaplains for South Africa; Rev. Sabelo Maseko, the Chief of Chaplains for Swaziland; and Captain Arnold Resnicoff, U.S. Navy Chaplain, in Swaziland (Provided photo)

I learned to war-game scenarios in all parts of my life—even carrying that over to the task of parenting, as my wife and I tried to teach our young daughter Malka that, while she should normally be respectful of others (especially "grown-ups") she should not hesitate to yell, kick, and scream if a stranger tried to take her away or force her into a car. It is hard to prepare those we love for danger, but as this book shows, it is a responsibility. And, as threats change, so must our planning.

We should always celebrate freedom, but never take it for granted – and that means not only reminding ourselves of past dangers, but of future threats as well. We openly practice our religion, but must—as this book shows—determine the best safeguards (from physical to electronic to new approaches to cybersecurity to protect information that might create vulnerabilities) to replace our old trap doors.

We must recognize the modern equivalents of the branches in the river that I took aim at in Vietnam. We must train ourselves to recognize signs of possible danger and take pre-emptive action, using good relationships with law enforcement to report suspicious behavior.

We must remember that just as an unlocked car or house is more likely to be the target of a break-in than one that is locked and protected, we must both improve areas where we are vulnerable—and work to project the message to would-be attackers and enemies that we are not the easy target they seek.

After Beirut, we created new ways to protect ourselves, including barriers to slow down vehicles before they reached our gates. We need to continue to learn from yesterday's attacks as we create security for today and tomorrow, but we also need to get better at imagining what new dangers we might face, preparing in advance for as many of them as possible.

We must love our country, and try our best to love our neighbor…but never forget that not all people are good. We must remember that hatred, prejudice, and racism may have threatened us with stones in the past, but the destructive power of hatred has multiplied with the power of new weapons. We must also remember that Houses of Worship—or places of prayer—have always been special targets, from the Tree of Life Synagogue, to the Ibrihimi Mosque, to the 16th Street Baptist Church in Birmingham.

Today it has become more and more common to say that "thoughts and prayers" don't help. I disagree. Granted, they are not *sufficient*, but they are *essential*. We should never stop thinking, praying, hoping—for better times, for less pain, for more joy…for others, and for ourselves. Our Houses of Worship should help us refine and strengthen our thoughts and our prayers in ways that help us act. But, as this extraordinarily important book by Dr. Bryen reminds us, first we must ensure that we pray in safety.

I pray that Dr. Bryen's book becomes an important guide for all religious communities. I pray that, with his help, we can pray in a safe and secure setting, and then—from our thoughts and prayer—our wisdom and faith can lay the foundation for lives that will create a better future for our community, our nation, and our world.

Rabbi Arnold E. Resnicoff naval career began with "Operation Game Warden" in Vietnam—the effort to keep the rivers free of Viet Cong infiltrators; continued with Naval Intelligence in Europe; and, after ordination as a rabbi, twenty-five years as US Navy chaplain. Following retirement, he served as National Director of Interreligious Affairs for the American Jewish Committee, and as Special Assistant for Values and Vision to the Secretary and Chief-of-Staff of the United States Air Force.

PREFACE

This book is for clergy, laymen and security experts who are concerned about security in holy places.

For convenience, I define a holy place as a place of worship, even if, as is many times the case, that the house of worship is tied to a school, a nursery, a senior center or even a community center.

The truth is that only a fraction of holy places in the United States are secure.

Most are open to all, which means worshipers and violent intruders.

Many are subject to external violence, everything from vandalism, arson, muggings and rapes or drive-by shootings.

Even the parking lots of holy places are at risk these days.

Whether a Christian church or assembly, a Mosque, Temple or a Synagogue, whether white or black or Asian or other ethnicity, everyone who goes to pray does so at risk.

And despite some declining attendance numbers, still many go to worship.

Among some 35 different Christian denominations there are over 100,000 local congregations with as many as 45 million worshipers.

For Jewish worshipers there are 3,727 synagogues.

There are 2,106 mosques in the United States and a Muslim population of around 3.15 million.

The United States has 7,498 Catholic schools in 2006-07, including 6,288 elementary schools and 1,210 secondary schools.

In total there are 2,320,651 students, including 1,682,412 students in the elementary/middle schools and 638,239 in high schools.

There are 861 Jewish day schools in the USA in 2013-2014, with an enrolment of 255,000 children from age 4 to grade 12.

There are hundreds of Christian, Jewish, Muslim and other camps in the United States, some day camps, some overnight. On top of that, many church groups sponsor retreats and adult study away from the city or town, often in summer camp grounds during the off season.

For all of them the risk of attack is growing. Holy Places are no longer safe.

In these pages I describe the danger in detail and offer a practical guide on how to strengthen security. A chapter is devoted to sources of government funding and how to apply for assistance. I also included a chapter on camps run by religious organizations, although the camps guide can easily be applied to any overnight or day camp. By the same token, many of the security proposals in this book can be adopted by others outside of religious organizations. The point of focus on places of worship is because security is, for most, sorely lacking.

Good organization is all important in assuring security for religious institutions, and good organization also means solid training for staff and security volunteers.

The decision on whether or not to have armed guards remains controversial. My view is armed guards are very important to head off an attack, although guards alone cannot guarantee the safety of a congregation.

The most important issue to be considered carefully is that unarmed guards and volunteers are risking their lives trying to provide security if the assailant is heavily armed and determined, as often is the case. It seems to me this is an ethical issue: it is wrong to put anyone in a position where they can't really defend themselves and could be killed.

At the end of the day, this is the issue that each congregation must decide for itself. But given the rise in levels of threat today, the time has come to take account of what is at stake and to act accordingly.

I want to thank everyone who kindly helped me in reading early drafts of this book and for offering suggestions on how to make it better.

My thanks go to Hyper-Speller of Word Refiner (www.wordrefiner.com) for its excellent work reviewing my manuscript. Hyper-Speller runs a terrific service that any author would appreciate.

Thanks also to Stanley Geftic, who applied his legal mind and dedication to systematically working through the text. His suggestions were invaluable.

Also my thanks to Andrew Apostolu, who made some important early suggestions that led me to reshape some of the chapters. Andrew and I come from completely opposite ends of the political spectrum, yet agree on the need for strong security for religious groups and institutions. Our collaboration illustrates that security is not, and should not be, based on one's politics. Nor should friendship, for that matter.

I want to thank Sussman Corporate Security for their support and encouragement. I serve as a senior advisor to the company.

All the errors that remain are my responsibility.

For those who want to contact me, please use the email author@securityforholyplaces.org.

Our new web page is www.securityforholyplaces.org. I will try to keep it updated. I also support a Facebook page for Security for Holy Places. The Facebook address is https://fb.me/SECHOLYPLACES

If you like the book, please leave a comment that we can post.

I hope what I have provided is worthwhile. While I cannot make any guarantee for security, even if every suggestion here is followed, I hope it helps provide all sanctuaries with a guide to assuring peaceful prayer and reflection.

You are invited to visit our website at www.securityforholyplaces.org

Stephen Bryen

Silver Spring, Maryland

CHAPTER 1

Guns, Gun Laws and Active Shooters

One of the most interesting facts is that most of the guns used in attacks on holy places or organizations tied to religious institutions are purchased legally in the United States.

In other parts of the world, especially where there are strong gun laws, guns are still plentiful. For example, terror groups in the UK, Germany, Belgium, Italy and elsewhere have got their weapons smuggled in by illegal gun dealers, providing weapons from Eastern Europe and Russia. In addition, there is a criminal underground at work in various countries manufacturing, or at least assembling guns, even automatic weapons, locally. For example, according to the London Daily Star[1], "Kyle Wood, 30, was chased down by armed National Crime Agency detectives during a raid in Hailsham, East Sussex. Wood was one of three men who built guns 'from scratch' in a warehouse on the industrial site - with guns produced there linked to two attempted murders." The recent attack on the synagogue in Halle, Germany and on a nearby Kabob shop featured what authorities say were home made guns including a shotgun and an automatic rifle.

Synagogue in Halle (Saale), Jüdischer Friedhof, Humboldtstraße (by Allexkoch [CC BY-SA 4.0])

Compared to most of the world, the United States has rather permissive gun laws. That does not mean that guns are not easily obtained in other countries.

For example, in nearby Mexico civilian gun ownership is illegal under Mexican law unless the owner purchases the weapon from a special shop run by the country's Department of Defense. But that does not seem to stop Mexico's infamous cartels from acquiring whatever weapons they want and to slaughter people pretty much at will. About 70% of those guns are bought legally in the United States and then smuggled into Mexico. Others are coming from Russia, China, Eastern Europe and the Middle East.

In the UK most modern guns are illegal, yet there is a distinct rise in shootings there.

In Canada, mostly every kind of gun except some for hunting are banned. Even pepper spray and other less-than-lethal chemicals, as well as Tasers™ can only be used by law enforcement. About 21 percent of murders in Canada were by handguns. Still others were killed by rifles and semiautomatic weapons. While Canada's rate is well-below the United States, it is a growing problem.

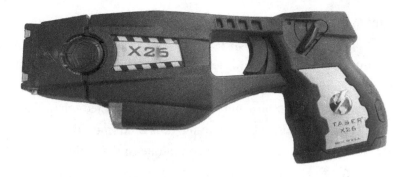

A Taser® (by ShareAlike 3.0 Unported CC BY-SA 3.0)

What makes the US different is the Second Amendment to the Constitution. It states that "A well-regulated Militia, being necessary to the security of a free state, the right of the people to keep and bear Arms, shall not be infringed."

Today, the closest thing we have to a militia might be the National Guard (which is organized under the authority of each state, but Guards can be federalized and used for both domestic law enforcement, as happened when there was racial strife in the south and for supporting US military operations abroad, as in Iraq and Afghanistan.) The National Guard formally is considered part of the US military reserve component.

But the National Guard differs in many respects from the citizen soldiers contemplated by America's Founding Fathers. The citizen soldier would come to the aid of his country when there was an emergency. He kept his kit and his gun or guns at home. In fact, the Founder's idea of a citizen reserve somewhat resembles the Israeli practice of reserves at home who can be summoned to battle and who also keep their weapons at home. Behind the US concept is the idea of resisting tyranny.

In any case, Federal and state governments have been nibbling at the intent of the Second Amendment for some time, trying to put restrictions on gun owners and gun ownership.

Concealed Carry

One restriction on a gun owner are "Concealed Carry" laws that are in place in cities and states around the country, but are not consistent from place to place.

Vermont won't issue permits for concealed carry. Others may, under certain circumstances issue such permits. Still others are directed to issue such permits, but sometimes do not. For more detailed information go to www.usacarry.com.

Most states will not issue a gun permit to any convicted felon. The Federal government also bars felons from owning guns or ammunition.

Specifically: the Federal rule is found in one of the main firearm statutes (18 USC § 922(g)(1)). It says that anyone "who has been convicted in any court of a crime punishable by imprisonment for a term exceeding one year" is barred from possessing a gun.

The only felonies that are not covered by the federal gun ban are:

- those "pertaining to antitrust violations, unfair trade practices, restraints of trade, or other similar offenses relating to the regulation of business practices," per 18 USC. § 921(a)(20)(A); and
- felony convictions from foreign countries, per Small v. United States (April 26, 2005)."[2]

But enforcement of this provision is not straightforward or simple.

There are two problems.

The first concerns whether states share information on convicted felons both with other states and with the Federal government. Some do, some try, and some don't. What this means is that a former convicted felon, let's say in Mississippi, may be able to buy a gun in Illinois simply because the data on his prior conviction in another state didn't get into the hands of the FBI. Similarly, military bases and organizations are supposed to share convicted felon information. In the past this has been hit or miss. This includes domestic and overseas military installations and bases.

The second concerns a legal gun owner who is subsequently convicted of a felony, serves time and then returns home. He may get a letter telling him (or her) to surrender his previously legally owned weapon, but while these letters are sometimes sent (assuming the person is still living at the same address and the demand letter reaches him or her), there isn't any follow up in most cases. You get a letter, you ignore it. So what?

These are not merely academic gaps in coverage. The case below shows how both of these gaps led to the deaths of five innocent people.

Gary Martin, who worked for the Henry Pratt Company in Aurora, Illinois brought his .40 calibre handgun to work because he knew he was going to be fired. He gunned down five co-workers. Back in 1995, he had been convicted of aggravated assault in Mississippi, a felony and served a prison term. Yet in 2014, he "successfully applied for an Illinois Firearm Owner's Identification (FOID) card" and bought a .40-caliber Smith & Wesson handgun.

When Martin tried to procure a concealed carry license that same year, the Mississippi conviction came up during a background check. Martin was denied a concealed carry license, police said, and his FOID card was revoked. Authorities never confiscated his gun.[3]

Law Enforcement Officer's Safety Act (LEOSA)

In 2004 Congress passed the Law Enforcement Officer's Safety Act (18 USC § 926), and thereafter twice amended the law. The purpose of the law is to allow active and retired (now called "separated from service") law enforcement officers to be allowed to carry firearms even if prohibited under any state or local laws.

For faith based organizations, this means that retired policemen, including military police and civilian police who worked for the federal government can carry weapons if they are "qualified," and therefore can be employed as armed security guards.

To be qualified, a separated from service individual would have to have left his or her service in good standing and have at least 10 years' experience as a law enforcement officer. In addition, the individual would have to have approved firearms training. Further provisions say that the person would not be qualified for reasons of mental health or found to be under the influence of alcohol or drugs.

The individual must carry a photographic identification issued by his previous law enforcement agency. Some states and some law enforcement organizations have refused to issue photographic identification, and a few court cases have taken up the issue.

At least one state, New Jersey requires that a separated service person also obtain a state carry permit, notwithstanding the LEOSA.

Qualified Law Enforcement officers may not carry hollow point bullets in jurisdictions where hollow point bullets are prohibited.

It is important for prospective hires to check the Photographic Identification Card and make sure it is valid. This can be done by contacting the issuing organization to confirm the authenticity of the ID card. Similarly, proof of firearms training should be requested.

Because a law enforcement officer can be separated from service sometimes because of an incident or incidents involving alleged irregularities (including misuse of firearms), but still be separated without penalty, it is important to carefully check the background of the individual and his or her prior service record.

Mental Illness

But perhaps the biggest problem are people suffering mental illness who get guns.

The Federal law on guns and persons with mental illness is very narrow and specific. It says that "Under 18 USC § 922(d), it is unlawful for any person to sell or otherwise dispose of any firearm or ammunition to any person knowing or having reasonable cause to believe that such person 'has been adjudicated as a mental defective or has been committed to any mental institution.'"

How would a gun seller know that a person had been "adjudicated as a mental defective" or know that a person had been previously committed to any mental institution?

Many states, like the Federal government have their own rules about mental illness and guns. Many of them are entirely subjective.

In Alabama the law says that a person of "unsound mind" should not be allowed to own a gun. An unsound mind is a euphemism for a mentally ill person. Who would make that judgement under Alabama law isn't clear.

California has its own twist. The law says a person that has been admitted to a [mental health] facility and is receiving inpatient treatment [for a mental disorder], is a danger to self or others, even though the patient has consented to that treatment. Of course, if a patient is in an institution he or she is not likely to be buying a gun.

In Maine, a person found not criminally responsible by reason of insanity of committing certain enumerated crimes cannot own a firearm.

And so it goes.

Mental health is a complex and difficult subject, and it is made even more opaque because in the United States disclosure of medical information is strictly controlled and limited.

The US has a law in place called the Health Insurance Portability and Accountability Act (HIPAA). It was originally formulated to help people keep their health insurance when they changed jobs or lost a job. But it is much more than that, and HIPAA today provides important guidelines on the disclosure of Personal Information that applies everywhere, from the doctor's office, to the hospital or clinic, to the insurance carrier, to the pharmacy and to the government. A key provision of is that Personal Health Information (PHI) must be protected.

PHI information includes:

- a patient's name, address, birth date and Social Security number;
- an individual's physical or mental health condition;
- any care provided to an individual; or
- information concerning the payment for the care provided to the individual that identifies the patient, or information for which there is a reasonable basis to believe could be used to identify the patient.

None of this can be disclosed unless the patient agrees or there is a court order. (There is apparently one important exception to disclosures of PHI. This involves a health business entity sharing information with its business partner(s) allegedly to help improve patient care. This matter became public when it was revealed that Google was aggregating PHI data from the health care provider Ascension. Google and Ascension claimed that such sharing was perfectly legal under HIPAA privacy guidelines. Individuals whose data was shared were not asked and did not give permission for the health care company to use their information. There were "furious" complaints raised over this matter, and it is likely that Congress will need to soon take up the issue and resolve whether this kind of sharing can be permitted, and if so under what circumstances and safeguards. This type of industry sharing is different than a doctor, medical testing laboratory or pharmacy sharing information on a patient without explicit consent.)

HIPAA imposes fines and even imprisonment for violation of its requirements. Transmittal of records (such as a doctor's prescription sent to a pharmacy) has to be done in a safe and secure way.

The question arises what can a doctor, psychiatrist, case worker or other professional disclose about the mental condition of a patient?

On July 20th, 2012 John Eagan Holmes entered the Century 16 movie theater in Aurora, Colorado, where a midnight showing of a new film called the "Dark Knight Rises" was screened. Holmes was carrying multiple weapons, set off tear gas grenades and killed 12 people and wounded 58, with a number of others hurt trying to escape.

Century 16 Movie Theater in Aurora, Colorado (By Algr -Went to nearby scene and took photo with my camera. Previously published: My facebook, CC BY-SA 3.0)

When the case came to trial, Holmes' attorneys argued that he was mentally ill and should not stand trial for murder. Two separate psychiatric examinations were done, but the court ruled that Holmes was competent to stand trial. Holmes was sentenced to life imprisonment without the possibility of parole when the jurors were divided over the death penalty (demanded by the prosecutor) because some of the jurors thought Holmes was insane.

Holmes had been enrolled at the Anshultz Medical campus of the University of Colorado, where he had been pursuing a PhD in neuroscience. He withdrew from the school not long before the shooting at the Aurora Theatre.

Dr. Lynne Fenton, a psychiatrist, was treating Holmes when he was a student at the University until he dropped out. Her medical notes on Holmes, along with the two court-appointed physicians' notes evaluating Holmes' sanity were released by the judge in 2018. Dr. Fenton did not think Holmes was a threat even though he was "silent and sullen" and she prescribed medication for him.

Even so, Dr. Fenton was worried about her patient. According to the Chicago Tribune, Dr. Fenton at Holmes' trial told the court "that Holmes told her he was having homicidal thoughts as often as three or four times a day, but never let on that he was building a weapons arsenal and planning a mass killing. If he revealed his intent, 'I likely would have put him on a mental health hold and contacted the police,' Fenton said."

Fenton then called his mother. She was told by the mother that he was shy and awkward for many years, "diminishing the apparent risk that he would be a danger to himself or others."

"I thought it was much less likely this was a sudden, new psychotic break," Fenton said. For that reason, she took no further action regarding Holmes.

The judge later said that "Holmes lost his patient-doctor privacy privileges when he argued a sanity defense. The judge permitted the Colorado Attorney General's Office to redact some portions of the reports to protect confidential testing information in sanity exams." But one of the reasons Fenton was testifying was the judge's finding.

Holmes was able to purchase his guns and ammunition legally and his mental health condition was never an issue. Even for the court, Holmes was found mentally capable of standing trial and the Court did not find him legally insane, meaning he was responsible for his actions, acted malevolently and knew the difference between right and wrong.

What would have happened had the University of Colorado psychiatrist decided Holmes was a threat? What should she have done?

In the real world, getting action even if there is very strong suspicion of suspected future violence, and even if the assessment is done by competent professionals, the chance for heading off a disaster is not too good.

To show how difficult these matters can be, consider the case of the Capital Gazette newspaper.

On Thursday, June 28th 2018 Jarrod Ramos carried out a mass shooting at the offices of the Capital Gazette newspaper in Annapolis, Maryland. Five employees died as a result of the attack.

The gunman used a pump-action 12-gauge shotgun, which had been purchased legally.

The newspaper office was on the ground floor of a shared facility and had a glass door entrance. There was no security guard either at the building or at the newspaper office.

While in high school, Ramos landed an internship with the super-secret National Security Agency (located nearby in Fort Meade, Maryland). Subsequently, he held other jobs and received top security clearances.

Ramos had a feud with the Capital Gazette that stretched back at least six years. A July 2011 article in the Gazette covered a criminal harassment charge against him, and in 2012 he filed a defamation lawsuit over the story against the paper and a columnist. The Circuit Court for Prince George's County ultimately dismissed the case. According to a police report released after the shooting, in 2013 representatives from the Gazette met with Anne Arundel County police to discuss Ramos' actions and threats against the newspaper. The officer meeting with the Gazette at the time wrote he "did not believe that Mr. Ramos was a threat to employees for [the newspaper]."

In a 2014 court filing, it was stated that Ramos threatened to kill Eric Hartley, the Capital Gazette columnist who had written about his harassment case. A Prince George's County judge ordered Ramos to stop posting about McCarthy on his Twitter account, but declined to order a mental evaluation.

But there is even more. Prior to the shooting Ramos had been treated five times for mental illness-related issues and he posted tweets and Facebook writings that were threatening. Ramos directed scores of profanity-laced tweets at the paper's journalists. At least one tweet was directed at columnist and Editor Rob Hiaasen, one of the victims killed when Ramos attacked the Capital Gazette office.

In a different tweet, Ramos said he'd enjoy seeing the paper stop publishing, but "it would be nicer" to see two journalists "cease breathing."

Ramos had sent a Facebook request out of the blue to a woman and thanked her for being the only person ever to say hello or be nice to him in school. The woman said she didn't remember Ramos, so he sent pictures. When she Googled him, she found they had gone to Anne Arundel High School in Maryland together. She wrote back to him because he was going through problems and she told him he should get help at a counseling center.

The woman said Ramos then sent months of emails in which he asked for help, called her vulgar names and told her to kill herself. He also emailed her company and tried to get her fired.

"She stopped writing back and told him to stop, but he continued. When she blocked him from seeing her Facebook page, he found things she wrote on other people's pages and taunted her with it, attaching screenshots of the postings to some of his emails." She called police, and for months he stopped. But then he started again, nastier than ever.

"All this without having seen her in person since high school. They never met until they came to court a couple of months ago."

Below are only two of many tweets. The community at large that knew Ramos thought he was crazy.

Jayne M-----
 @j-----
Woman tells me she was with Jarrod Ramos when he saw court commissioner Thursday after fatal shooting at Capital Gazette (she was

def[endant]) [sic] in unrelated case) Says he was making racial slurs at black officers.. and was "spazzing out"
9:21 AM - Jun 29, 2018

Jayne M-----

✔@j-----

"He's a f***** nut job" --woman who says she was stalked by suspect in fatal shooting of 5 people at Capital Gazette in Annapolis...says she warned former police official years ago.. ."he will be your next mass shooter"
8:45 PM - Jun 28, 2018

---

*(Twitter text above reproduced above as it appeared with errors but the full name of the sender and Twitter address has been removed and inappropriate language has been replaced with *****)*

No matter. Despite pleas to law enforcement and to a local court, Ramos was free to do what he wanted to do. And despite his record of treatment for mental problems, Ramos had no problem buying guns legally.

Annapolis is the state capital of Maryland. It is a beautiful town, not far from Washington, DC and quite sophisticated, with a highly-educated talent base and located not far from the National Security Agency headquarters and the city of Baltimore. Even so, the "system" proved unable to contain the threat, or even to adequately acknowledge it.

There are certainly dozens, if not hundreds, of Ramos-type cases around the country. The foggy line between an unhappy person and a mental ill person must be recognized. Furthermore, from what we know of active shooter events, many of them at workplaces, but also even at churches and synagogues, such people are a source of threat that cannot be disregarded.

A Baptist Church is Shot Up

Devin Patrick Kelley was a violent man. He was convicted while serving in the US Air Force for domestic violence. He was tried by military court martial for assaulting his wife and fracturing the head of his stepson. Kelley made death threats against the superior officers who charged him, and he was caught sneaking firearms onto Holloman Air Force Base in New Mexico. Around that same time, he made threats to a coworker. He was then admitted to Peak Behavioral Health Services, a mental health[4] facility in Santa Teresa, New Mexico. He escaped at least once from the Peak Behavioral Health facility.

The facility's director of military affairs later recalled that Kelley had stayed at the facility for several weeks, until he was brought to court martial. While there, he had expressed a desire for "some kind of retribution to his chain of command" and was discovered to have used computers to order "weapons and tactical gear to a P.O. Box in San Antonio."

Kelley and his wife divorced in October 2012. In an interview with *Inside Edition*[5], his ex-wife said she lived in constant fear of him, as their marriage was filled with abuse. He once threatened her at gunpoint over a speeding ticket, and later threatened to kill her and her entire family.

Kelley was brought before a general court martial[6] on four charges: assault on his wife, aggravated assault on his stepson, two charges of pointing a loaded gun at his wife, and two counts of threatening his wife with an unloaded gun. In November 2012, Kelley pleaded guilty to two counts of Article 128 Uniform Code of Military Justice (UCMJ), for the assault of his wife and stepson. In return, the weapons charges were dropped.

After he served his time and returned home, Kelley was investigated for sexual assault and rape, and for a physical assault of his then new girlfriend. The Comal County (Texas) Sheriff's Office did not bring charges against Kelley, and "the case became inactive because the victim did not respond to four follow-up calls and messages from a sheriff's office detective."

Kelley also received a suspended sentence in Texas for cruelty to animals.

Despite his prior felony conviction in the Air Force, Kelley lied about his background to pass a background check and obtained a license from the Texas Department of Public Safety[7] as a security guard.

On the night of October 31, less than a week before the shooting on November 5, 2017, Kelley attended a festival at the Sutherland Springs First Baptist Church wearing all black. According to two parishioners who were at the festival, he acted so strangely that people had to keep an eye on him. One also examined him to make sure he was not carrying a firearm.

Stephen Willeford, former NRA firearms instructor who fired upon and injured the shooter
(Official White House Photo by Tia Dufour)

Kelley's estranged second wife sometimes attended the First Baptist Church with her family. Prior to the shooting, he sent threatening text messages to her mother. His wife and her mother were not at the church when the attack occurred, but he killed his wife's grandmother at the church.

The Church in Sutherland Springs was unprotected.

Kelley legally purchased two guns (a European-American Armory Windicator® .38-caliber revolver and a 9 mm SIG Sauer P250 pistol) from the Holloman Air Force Base Exchange. These purchases took place before he was charged with domestic abuse.

Kelley later purchased four guns, including a 9 mm Glock 19 pistol, a .22-caliber Ruger SR22 pistol, a Ruger GP100 .357 Magnum revolver and a Ruger AR-556 rifle, at stores in Colorado and Texas between 2014 and 2017. The AR-556 comes in different models, although the manufacturer advertises it as a sporting rifle. Some models hold 10 rounds; others 30 rounds. Kelley's held 30 rounds per magazine.

Kelley's Ruger AR-556 Assault Rifle (Photo Credit: Sensei Alan, Wiki, Creative Commons 2.0)

Kelley simply lied on his application about prior convictions. But, when he tried to get a concealed carry permit from the State of Texas, he was turned down because of his prior convictions.

According to news reports, Kelley's conviction in the US Air Force was not communicated to the FBI's National Crime Information Center (NCIC). Thus he was able to legally buy guns in Colorado and Texas, since gun shops typically run NCIC checks to see if the purchase can be approved.

The National Crime Information Center is the nation's most extensive criminal justice information system and is maintained by the Federal Bureau of Investigation (FBI). NCIC contains over 24 million records in 14 files and provides user agencies with information on items such as missing and wanted persons, stolen vehicles, and criminal history records. Over 19,000 law enforcement and other criminal justice agencies in the United States and Canada can access NCIC through their computer systems. The Center was established in 1967.

Gun dealers hand a prospective purchaser a form to fill out which includes prior arrest and related information, but the form often is not audited. Next the dealer calls the Center or, if he has an authorized terminal does so electronically. According to the FBI, more than 230 million checks have been made by gun shop cashiers prior to a purchase and more than 1.3 million denials have been issued since the system was put in place. The applicant must still meet state requirements—such as age requirements. In at least one state (South Carolina), if you have previously legally purchased a gun, the NCIC check is waived.

When Kelley entered the church, he yelled, "Everybody die, [expletives]!" as he proceeded up and down the aisle and shot at people in the pews.

Police found 15 empty magazines capable of each holding 30 rounds. According to investigators, the shooting was captured on a camera set up at the back of the church to record regular services for uploading online. The footage shows Kelley methodically shooting the victims, pausing only to reload his rifle.

Stephen Willeford, a former NRA firearms instructor, challenged Kelley when he left the church in the church's parking lot. He managed to shoot him a number of times, but Kelley sped off in his pickup truck and was chased. He crashed it and apparently shot himself in the head.

Twenty-six people in the church were killed, including an unborn child, and twenty more were wounded.

Charleston Bible Class Shooting

On June 17, 2015 Dylann Roof took his Glock pistol and killed nine black congregants at the Charleston, South Carolina Emanuel African Methodist Episcopal Church while they were conducting a bible study class. Roof was able to buy his gun because of a "clerical error" in the NCIC clearance system. Roof had a prior felony arrest for dealing drugs. The NCIC had an entry there was an arrest and while Roof waited the mandatory three-day period before being granted a gun permit, the FBI failed to provide any details to the gun dealer. As a result, Roof was cleared by default and bought the Glock pistol.

Christchurch Mosque Shootings

Brenton Tarrant was 28 years old at the time he carried out mass shootings at the Al Noor Mosque in Riccarton, a suburb of Christchurch, New Zealand and at the Linwood Islamic Center, 5 km (3 miles) from the al-Noor Mosque. The attacks took place on the 15th of March, 2019. Tarrant planned to go on to attack a mosque in Ashburn, or a child care center belonging to the al-Noor community. He did not get to attack the other locations but was arrested approximately 21 minutes after the first emergency call to police.

Tarrant, an Australian citizen and known white supremacist, had at least two semi-automatic rifles and two shotguns, plus 1 lever action rifle. He bought the guns legally starting in December, 2017 and got around Australian magazine clip size restrictions by acquiring large capacity clips (30 rounds per magazine) separately.

There were no guards at either mosque. There also appears to have been no security system at either location.

Tarrant entered the al Noor Mosque at 1:40 PM through the front door and began shooting for about 6 minutes.

At 1:55 PM he tried to enter the front door of the Linwood Mosque, but initially was unable to do so, so he started firing through windows at the worshippers. As some escaped he entered the front door and continued firing.

One of his guns was equipped with a powerful strobe light, the object of which was to confuse and/or temporarily blind his victims.

Tarrant was equipped with a body camera and live-streamed the first 17 minutes of his attacks on Facebook Live. Just prior to starting his first assault, he released what he called "The Great Replenishment" manifesto, which he sent by email to leading government officials and broadcast on social media.

Tarrant killed 51 persons (47 male, 4 female) and wounded another 49.

It was the worst terror attack ever in New Zealand.

Tarrant pled not guilty in a preliminary hearing. His trial is scheduled for June, 2020.

Yom Kippur Synagogue Attack

Yom Kippur, the Day of Atonement, is the most solemn Jewish holiday of the year. In Germany, intelligence officials had warned that there was great danger of attacks on Jews and Jewish institutions during the Rosh Hashanah (Jewish New Year) and Yom Kippur religious days. Outside of Israel, in 2019 Rosh Hashanah is celebrated starting at sundown, September 29th and ending at sundown on October 1st. Yom Kippur began on Sunday, October 8th at sundown and concluded at sundown on October 9th. (In Israel, Rosh Hashanah is celebrated only on one day.)

Halle is a small eastern German town. Most of the Jews who lived in the town prior to World War II were shipped off by the Nazis to concentration camps. The original synagogue was destroyed, but the adjacent Moorish-style building, used as a chapel to the adjoining cemetery, survived and is now the synagogue for the town's Jews, most of whom are post USSR emigrants from Russia.

A young neo-Nazi named Stephen Balliet attacked the Halle synagogue on the day of Yom Kippur. He was armed with a shotgun, said to have been home constructed, and a semi-automatic weapon (called a Luty submachine gun, but it may have been a homemade version or one made by criminal gangs for sale) along with grenades, small pipe bombs and Molotov Cocktails. He wore combat clothes and a ballistic helmet on which was mounted a small camera. Part of his attack (with audio) was live-streamed over Amazon's Twitch live-streaming network. The video was removed a few hours after the attack.

The video reveals that his sub-machine gun jammed four times, preventing him from shooting a passer-by who then ran away.

Balliet tried to enter the synagogue main door. While the synagogue did not have any guards, armed or otherwise, it did have a CCTV camera system watching the outer-perimeter, and it was actively monitored. When Balliet was seen approaching the synagogue, the doors were hastily barricaded (in addition to being locked). There were about 80 congregants inside, including 10 Americans.

There are two entrances to this synagogue—an entrance by the front door and an entrance on the side facing into the cemetery. The cemetery is protected by a 5 or 6 foot wall, and the entrance to it by an iron gate that was locked.

Balliet used his shotgun to try and blast open the front door (from photos it appears he fired two or three rounds). He next tried placing an explosive to blast the door open, but it failed. He left an active explosive by the front door and tried to break into the side entrance gate, but failed. He was challenged by a woman walking down the street –he shot her in the back and she died on the spot.

From the synagogue he headed to a nearby Turkish-owned Kabob shop while he was ranting about Jews, Turks and Feminists (heard on the audio feed). At the Kabob shop he fired his rifle from outside that struck and killed a man inside. The others ran to the back of the shop looking for an exit, but some hid in a bathroom in the back. In any case, Balliet did not pursue them and angrily pumped more bullets into the already dead victim. He then ran from the scene. He was later apprehended by police where he appears to have been hurt when the taxi he hijacked crashed into a truck.

No one yet knows how Balliet got his weapons and bombs.

But the bigger question is how come the German government, knowing there were acute threats to Jewish institutions, failed to provide any guards. In Germany, private guards (with one exception) are not allowed to be armed.

Red Flag Laws

Red Flag Laws, also known as **Extreme Risk Protection Orders** are in place in some US states, and President Donald Trump has urged their expansion. The idea of the Red Flag Law is to allow a family member (and in some cases others) to petition a court to restrain the person alleged to be an extreme risk and take possession of his or her weapons.

So far, twelve states and the District of Columbia have enacted such laws allowing family or household members, in addition to law enforcement officers, to petition a state court to declare a person "in the throes of a crisis" unfit to have guns.

Gifford's Law Center reports (at the time of writing) that the states with Red Flag laws are:

- California
- Colorado
- Delaware (Only law enforcement can petition for *ex parte* orders)
- Hawaii (effective January 1, 2020)
- Illinois
- Maryland
- Massachusetts
- Nevada (effective January 1, 2020)
- New Jersey
- New York
- Oregon
- Washington

As will be readily apparent, in the case of the Aurora, Colorado shooter and the Maryland Capital Gazette shooter, there was no family member that stepped forward. One presumes that the psychiatrist treating James Holmes could have contacted the police had she thought he was "in the throes of a crisis", but she did not. Similarly, in Maryland no family member contacted the police, and when people threatened by the Capital Gazette shooter went to law enforcement and the courts, their complaint was effectively turned down.

There are many questions that likewise arise as to the impact on an individual's rights under the law in such circumstances, and the possibility that the courts could be used to deny gun rights because of family disputes or other similar matters. Even law enforcement could potentially use such laws as a way of causing harm to people that they dislike or oppose. In short, there are some serious civil rights issues connected with Red Flag laws that remain to be explored.

Who are Active Shooters? Below is the US Secret Service assessment and some additional observations that may prove helpful. According to the US Secret Service[8]:

- Nearly half active shooter events were motivated by a personal grievance related to a workplace, domestic, or other issue
- Over half had histories of criminal charges, mental health symptoms, and/or illicit substance use or abuse
- All had at least one significant stressor within the last five years, and over half had indications of financial instability in that timeframe
- Over three-quarters made concerning communications and/or elicited concern from others prior to carrying out their attacks. On average, those who did elicit concern caused more harm than those who did not.

Here are some additional observations by the author:
- How many were mentally ill isn't known and in any case difficult to determine because mental illness is defined in different ways by states and local governments.
- Most of the well-known cases involving active shooters and gun violence were cases where the guns were purchased legally (even if the purchaser lied on government-supplied forms to get them), or the shooter purchased the weapons before the person was convicted of a felony or before he or she was known to have been treated for an emotional or mental problem or where the treatment for mental health was not reported to the State or FBI (per HIPAA regulations).

What Does this Mean for Places of Worship and Religious Institutions?

Places of worship and religious institutions should report all threats to the police and to the FBI without exception.

A direct threat is where someone explicitly and in a public way makes a threat against a person or an organization or institution.

An indirect threat is a more generalized threat to a category of persons or institutions, such as all churches or all Catholics, or all Blacks, or all Jews.

Sometimes these threats come in the form of a mail threat; sometimes it is a phone call, and other times it is on social media.

Monitoring social media is a very difficult task, but it would be a great help if social media promptly reported threats not only to the police but also to people who would be impacted by the threat.

While some social media outlets are beginning to cull users who threaten some form of violence, this is not universally the case nor is there any legal requirement for social media operators to do so. One of the problems is the nexus between threats (which may be political and social but not necessarily intending violence) and First Amendment freedom of speech guarantees in the US Constitution.

Social media is starting to deal with some generic threats, for example Facebook says it will block Facebook pages and users who support antisemitism, Facebook won't do that for holocaust denial, even though holocaust deniers are almost always antisemitic.

Facebook does not monitor personal threats, or even have a way of flagging them (or so it appears). It gets even worse on other social media, which do nothing when it comes to threats of violence.

Many of the active shooter cases involve social media "manifestos" of would-be killers.

John T. Earnest, the 19 year-old shooter who killed a woman and wounded three others at the Chabad Poway Synagogue in California posted a hate-filled manifesto on social media before he committed the crime.

In the Pittsburgh Tree of Life synagogue shooting, Robert Bowers, who killed eleven worshipers and wounded another six, posted to a highly controversial website called GAB, an English-language social media website, launched in 2017.

He wrote:

Robert Bowers @onedingo
2 hours ago

HIAS likes to bring invaders in that kill our people.

I can't sit by and watch my people get slaughtered.

Screw your optics, I'm going in.

∧   ● Comments   ↻ Repost   ❝ Quote

Tweet from Robert Bowers

HIAS is the Hebrew International Aid Society and like other religiously-based organizations such as Lutheran World Services, provides help to immigrants.

GAB, according to the New York Times[9] has "become a haven for white nationalists, neo-Nazis and other extremists."

A Florida man was arrested for threatening to kill minorities, including Jews. Joshua John Leff, 40, was arrested on June 14th, 2019 at his home in Fort Myers and charged with intimidation, sending written threats to kill and possession of a weapon by a convicted felon. He made the threats on social media sites Bitchute and Gab, the Florida Department of Law Enforcement said in a statement. "The department began its investigation after receiving a tip about Leff's statements and videos inciting violence against minority groups including blacks, Jews, and gays," according to The Times of Israel[10].

The Times of Israel also called attention to "Cesar Sayoc, Jr., the suspect in the pipe bomb mailing campaign, who had a history of posting hateful and violent messages[11] on Facebook and Twitter that were laced with misinformation and conspiracy theories."

Social media also has played a huge role in radicalizing extremists who then carry out acts of terrorism on behalf of ISIS, al-Qaeda and other foreign and domestic organizations. Even though the FBI has testified about how terrorist groups use social media, compliance by social media outlets so far is voluntary and most continue to allow posting of hate speech and allow terror groups access to their sites.

Since 2017, Facebook has issued a manual on credible threats of violence and more recently has started removing posts, but it seems to be far from universally applied and active shooters are still posting grievances and manifestos on Facebook and other social media.

In at least one important court case, a federal judge in San Francisco "dismissed a lawsuit filed by family members and victims of the 2015 mass shooting in San Bernardino, California that accused Facebook, Google and Twitter of knowingly supporting ISIS and helping the group spread its radical beliefs."

The judge wrote that while the three social media giants were "generally aware that ISIS used their services, there is no evidence that they 'intended to further' the group's terrorist activity."

Any right-minded person would think that the judge made a big mistake and this issue will have to be revisited. But until it is, the judge's decision forms a strong precedent protecting social media providers even when terrorism is involved.

One point that is glaringly obvious is that federal authorities often are unwilling to upset the applecart when it comes to strongly vested interests such as American social media corporations. For that reason, privacy cases, especially those involving Google's Gmail have been decided against the interest of those whose email information may have been compromised.

All of this makes monitoring social media very difficult and the difficulty is compounded when the government and its judges fail to understand the threat posed by individuals and groups promoting hate and violence on the Internet.

For churches, synagogues, mosques and temples this makes it especially challenging since they won't have any warning unless someone in the community or local law enforcement spots a high-risk threat.

Many church leaders think that they can stay in touch with local law enforcement and the FBI and that this will give them ample warning if there is an active threat.

The underlying and often wrong assumption is that local law enforcement and the FBI are all-knowing and are adequately staffed to carry out extensive data mining across social media and other information sources.

There are very few cases of an actual active shooter where the FBI had prior warning, or where the warning was specific enough for anything more than a general warning (if that).

There is a reluctance of law enforcement to raise levels of community anxiety without very strong justification and evidence.

Not all statements and manifestos use the real name of the person or group posting them. This makes accurate identification a challenge.

And the FBI is not able to monitor all social media or has sufficient human or electronic intelligence capabilities to spot a threat before it materializes.

Moreover, not all threats manifest themselves in ways that are detectable, even if the resources existed to survey all social media and threatening emails. Even where a threat is reported, the FBI and local law enforcement may not believe they have enough information to take any action. And there is always the chance in such circumstances they are being fed false information aimed at trying to ruin someone's reputation or to divert law enforcement from a "real" threat.

Some terrorist organizations often make many threats and boasts that are posted on social media, including Twitter. Which of these threats will be carried out is anyone's guess.

While everyone should always take any warning from law enforcement with utmost seriousness (more about that later on how to prepare), it is a mistake to think there will always be warnings or the warnings will be specific enough to be immediately actionable.

The following are guidelines on threats:

- Take all threats seriously and engage law enforcement and other help to avoid any potentially harmful incident
- Stay close to local law enforcement and take their guidance and advice
- Get security briefings from the FBI and try to make sure as many members of the congregation as possible can attend these briefings
- If you receive a threatening email or voice call, report it at once. If you have voicemail or other recording equipment, save the threatening call recording for law enforcement and for possible legal intervention

Just because you report it, don't think law enforcement is going to help you or even has the manpower to cover you against a threat. More than likely police and FBI will launch some sort of investigation, but you may never hear anything more about it from the authorities.

- If you see individuals lurking outside your church, synagogue or mosque, report it immediately. If you have a mobile phone snap a photo of the persons lurking. If there is a camera surveillance system save photos and video on the system and, if a vehicle is involved see if there is a picture of their vehicle and best of all, a photo showing the vehicle's license plate
- Don't expect there will always be a warning
- Take steps to secure both the perimeter and interior of your building(s) (more on this subject later)
- Remind your congregants that if they get any kind of threat it should be reported to the leaders of the congregation and to law enforcement

- Take workplace grievances seriously and manage them as sympathetically as possible
- Remember that in many cases active shooters will attack using semi-automatic weapons, particularly assault-type rifles, pump action shotguns or semi-automatic handguns
- While you should report cases of strange behavior and perceived mental illness, the chances are that the authorities may find it difficult to act in ways that will protect your institution
- Gun laws do not really do much to protect citizens from gun violence or, put another way, existing gun laws often fail to afford protection from gun crime

---

Don't trust your luck. Be prepared!

CHAPTER 2

Bombs, Bombing & Stabbings

A ctive Shooters sometimes also carry bombs or plant bombs, but sometimes bombers operate without being active shooters.

Since the 19th century there have been church bombings in the United States. At least one of them, back in 1963, successfully targeted the Sixteenth Street Baptist Church in Birmingham, Alabama. The church was predominantly attended by black Americans and it also was a meeting place for civil rights leaders. Four young girls were killed and many other people injured.

A history of the incident by History Channel reports: "KKK [Ku Klux Klan, white supremacist hate group, whose primary target is African Americans] members had routinely called in bomb threats intended to disrupt civil rights meetings as well as services at the church.

"At 10:22 a.m. on the morning of September 15, 1963, some 200 church members were in the building—many attending Sunday school classes before the start of the 11 am service—when the bomb detonated on the church's east side, spraying mortar and bricks from the front of the church and caving in its interior walls."

16th Street Baptist church bombing 1963 (© Associated Press, By Permission)

"Most parishioners were able to evacuate the building as it filled with smoke, but the bodies of four young girls (14-year-old Addie Mae Collins, Cynthia Wesley and Carole Robertson and 11-year-old Denise McNair) were found beneath the rubble in a basement restroom."

This was the third bombing in eleven days in September, 1963 in Alabama, all of it related to civil rights and the court-ordered integration of schools.

Enforcement was slow and difficult. The History Channel report goes on to say: "Klan leader Robert E. Chambliss was brought to trial for the bombings and convicted of murder. Continuing to maintain his innocence, Chambliss died in prison in 1985."

"The case was again reopened in 1980, 1988 and 1997, when two other former Klan members, Thomas Blanton and Bobby Frank Cherry, were finally brought to trial; Blanton was convicted in 2001 and Cherry in 2002. A fourth suspect, Herman Frank Cash, died in 1994 before he could be brought to trial."

In addition to church bombings and burnings in the south, other bombings involved church leaders.

On January 17, 2011 in Spokane, Washington there was an attempt to bomb a Memorial March for Martin Luther King, with a radio-controlled shrapnel-filled pipe bomb that also was stuffed with rat poison, to make it hard to stop victims' bleeding. (Rat poison is Coumadin, which acts in small doses as a blood thinner and in large doses to kill rats who, when ingesting the poison, bleed internally and die.) The bomber also put human faeces in the bomb, hoping to cause disease in the victims if they survived the bomb and rat poison.

The bomb was discovered at the parade grounds and was verified by bomb-sniffing dogs and disarmed. The bomb itself, hidden inside a backpack, was sent to the FBI's laboratory at Quantico, Virginia.

The bomber was a white supremacist named Kevin Harpham. He was arrested, tried and sentenced to 32 years in prison.

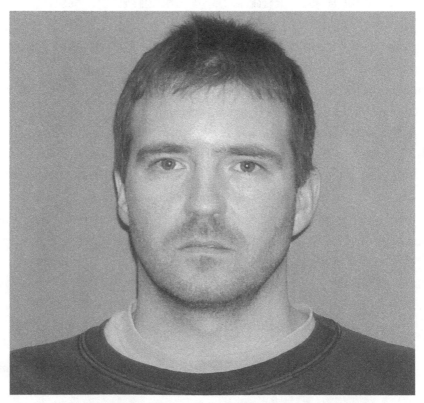

Kevin W. Harpham.(Booking photo from the U.S. Marshals Service.)

Holy Place Bombings

There are many different types of bombs, many of them homemade devices. Some use commercial explosives, some are home-brew explosives and others use sophisticated, "plastic" explosives that are hard to detect. Some explosives are stolen from military bases, construction companies and other legitimate users. Others are smuggled into the United States from foreign sources originating often in Eastern Europe and the Middle East.

Sri Lanka Church Bombings

The recent attacks on Sir Lankan churches helps us understand how bombs are made and used.

Sri Lanka's suicide bombers are thought to have used TATP, chemically known as triacetone triperoxide, an explosive made from commonly available household ingredients including nail polish remover—acetone—and hydrogen peroxide—a bleach.

The eight or more suicide bombers in Sri Lanka must have purchased large amounts of these two ingredients, yet despite being on the police "radar screen," no one picked it up. According to news reports, it is suspected they made the explosives in a copper factory in Wellampitiya, a suburb of Colombo.

The factory was owned by Inshaf Ahamad, who is believed to have blown himself up at the Shangri-La Hotel in Colombo.

Middle-class bombers

While the full scale of the conspiracy is not yet known, the suicide bombers appear to have been successful middle-class people. The father of Inshaf Ahamad is known as a successful spice trader and he was arrested after bombs in his home went off, killing three policemen.

It has long been the case that many top terrorists are, in fact, successful entrepreneurs or professionals, including doctors and dentists such as George Habash, known as al-Hakim, or "the doctor," who was educated at the American University in Beirut.

He famously headed the Popular Front for the Liberation of Palestine[12] (PFLP) and also for a time headed the PLO (Palestine Liberation

Organization). Likewise, Yasser Arafat who headed the PLO later, was a university graduate and came from a middle-class family.

But perhaps the most famous was Osama Bin Laden[13], who came from a well-connected and influential family of millionaires in Saudi Arabia tied to the country's rapidly expanding construction industry. Bin Laden attended the secular Al-Thager Model School and King Abdul-Aziz University. He studied business administration and had a degree in civil engineering.

Bin Laden would go on to mastermind the use of aircraft as bombs in the horrendous September 11, 2001(9/11) attacks in the United States (New York Twin Trade Towers, Washington's Pentagon and a commercial aircraft destroyed in Pennsylvania probably heading for the US Capitol). All included, 2,996 people died in the Bin Laden organized attacks aimed at the critical economic, military and political nerve centers of the United States.

Manchester Arena Bombing

TATP plus shrapnel was used in the Manchester suicide bombing[14] in 2017 that killed 23 people and wounded another 39. The bomber was Salman Ramadan Abedi, a local man of Libyan ancestry who was 22 years old.

Floral tributes to the victims of the attack in St Ann's Square in Manchester city center
(Wikipedia, Creative Commons)

More than half of those killed were women and children. Abedi was previously reported to police as an extremist, but police did not regard him as a high risk despite a clear background of fighting with Islamic Jihadists in Libya.

Abedi had attended the University of Salford, but dropped out. Previously, he had been a fighter with his father in Libya and ironically was rescued in 2014 by the Royal Navy, who extracted him and other British citizens from Tripoli. He had been fighting with an Islamic radical group.

According to police reports, it is believed Abedi made the TATP explosive himself, but brought triggering material with him from Libya, probably supplied by a Salafist Jihadist organization connected to ISIS (the Islamic State of Iraq and the Levant).

On March 22, 2016, there were two suicide bombings at the Brussels Zaventem airport and another at the Maalbeek Metro station in central Brussels. Thirty-two people died in these attacks and more than 300 were injured.

The airport bombs were carried in two large suitcases and the Maalbeek Metro bombing took place on a train. The bombs were made up of TATP and shrapnel.

The Brussels terrorists were directly connected to the 2015 attacks in Paris that included the Bataclan Theatre and the Stade de France football (soccer) stadium in Saint-Denis. At the stadium there were three explosions set off by suicide bombers, another explosion took place on a Paris street, and at the Bataclan, the terrorists blew themselves up with suicide vests after police finally broke through. The Bataclan terrorists carried automatic weapons.

All the explosive materials were TATP.

ISIS was directly responsible for the Brussels and Paris attacks and for the Manchester suicide bombing. ISIS has already taken credit for the Sri Lanka attacks.

TATP has also been showing up elsewhere, including in the United States. A Florida man named Jared Coburn, 37-years-old at the time of his arrest, was making TATP in his home. He also had other explosives in the home.

A member of the Volusia County Sheriff's Office holds an electrical switch device, part of the "bomb-making paraphernalia" recovered from a home in Lake Helen, Fla., where the explosive TATP was also found. (Volusia County Sheriff's Office)

TATP is extraordinarily volatile and many ISIS, Hamas, Hezbollah and other terrorists have blown themselves up handing TATP. In other cases, they escaped death, but were badly wounded. Israelis call these "work accidents."

Most standard bomb sensing equipment cannot detect TATP, but new sensors are being introduced that use colorimetric sensor arrays[15] – essentially sensing the temperature of TATP released gases. TATP also gives off a fairly strong odor of decomposing fruit.

Boston Marathon Bombing

The 2013 Boston Marathon bombers took a different tact. They put explosives and ball bearings inside pressure cookers and exploded them remotely in the midst of the marathon race.

Pressure cooker bombs include the 2006 Mumbai train bombings[16], 2010 Stockholm bombings[17] (failed to explode), the 2010 Times Square car bombing attempt[18] (failed to explode), and the 2017 Manchester Arena bombing[19]. On Canada Day[20] 2013, pressure cooker bombs failed to explode at the Parliament Building in Victoria, British Columbia.

In 2004 the Department of Homeland Security said this about pressure cooker bombs:

"Typically, these bombs are made by placing TNT or other explosives in a pressure cooker and attaching a blasting cap at the top of the pressure cooker. The size of the blast depend on the size of the pressure cooker and the amount of explosive placed inside"

"Pressure-cooker bombs are made with readily available materials and can be as simple or as complex as the builder decides. These types of devices can be initiated using simple electronic components including, but not limited to, digital watches, garage-door openers, cell phones or pagers. As a common cooking utensil, the pressure cooker is often overlooked when searching vehicles, residences or merchandise crossing the U.S. borders."

The Boston Marathon bombers set off their bombs, left inside backpacks, near the finish line of the race, remotely using a cellular phone-linked device to ignite an explosive cap, which triggered the explosives inside the pressure cooker. There are reports that the explosive material put into the pressure cookers was extracted from commercial fireworks.

Pressure cooker bombs are classified as IEDs—that is Improvised Explosive Devices.

Even large bombs, that use fertilizer and propane to "boost" their explosive power, are types of IEDs. Because these bombs require a significant amount of space, they are often found packed into trucks or vans. The boosting material can be fertilizer or propane gas tanks. (In the Middle East, many IEDs are also made from conventional bombs that are strapped together and set off with a small explosion, usually the bomb is buried or hidden in the ground or placed up against buildings.)

Bombed out Alfred P. Murrah Federal Building in downtown Oklahoma City, Oklahoma, April 19, 1995
(by Staff Sergeant Preston Chasteen, US Department of Defense)

In the famous Oklahoma City bombing, Timothy McVeigh and Terry Nichols mixed 5,000 pounds of ammonium nitrate fertilizer, 1,200 pounds of liquid nitromethanes (used as industrial solvents) and 350 pounds of Tovex Blastrite®[21] Gel, which McVeigh allegedly stole from a rock quarry. All of this was put into a Ryder Rental truck that the conspirators modified to support the bomb and set up a time-delay fuse system so they could get away from the truck. When the blast went off, it destroyed the Alfred P. Murrah Federal Building and killed more than 168 people, injuring another 680. Unfortunately, nineteen of the victims were infants and young children because the Federal building supported a day care center located toward the front of the structure.

Tovex is regarded as a modern replacement for TNT (dynamite). It is a water-gel explosive composed of ammonium nitrate and methyl ammonium nitrate. It is considered safer to use on construction and mining sites than TNT.

Bombs in backpacks, suitcases or bags are found worldwide. The Sri Lankan bombers carried explosive backpacks and the Manchester Arena bomber in 2017 likewise either carried a backpack or had the bomb taped to his body. The bomb was stuffed with nails and glass. Twenty-two people died and another 250 were injured at the Manchester Arena.

IMPORTANT: Check backpacks particularly on strangers seeking to enter your facility. Consider a policy of not admitting persons carrying backpacks or large bags or parcels.

The Manchester suicide bomber, the Sri Lankan bombers, the Boston Marathon bombers and possibly McVeigh and Nichols in Oklahoma City were all previously known to law enforcement and to intelligence agencies.

In Sri Lanka, there were multiple warnings from "foreign" intelligence services including the United States' CIA, but the authorities both failed to act and failed to warn church goers and the hotels that were targeted by the terrorists. The attacks definitely were religiously motivated and the Sri Lankan terrorist cells were tied to ISIS.

In the Boston Marathon bomb case, the FBI received warnings from Russian security about the Tsarnaev brothers (Tamerlan and Dzhokhar) in March, 2011 (the two perpetrators that are known, there could have been others), and the FBI actually interviewed their mother, Zubeidit, in Boston, and Customs and Border Patrol agents interviewed Tamerlan Tsarnaev. After the interviews, the FBI closed the matter in June, 2011 and did not pursue it again. Again, in September, 2011 the Russians cabled the CIA and repeated their concern about the Tsarnaev's.

In 2012, Tamerlan traveled to Russia and was a subject of Russian surveillance. The Russians alleged that the two brothers were connected with militant Islamists. Tamerlan was on the US "no fly" list, but no one paid attention. He spent six months in Russia before returning to the United States and he was reportedly in the company of well-known Islamic radicals.

It didn't matter.

Neither the FBI nor CIA or, for that matter the Boston police did anything until after the bombing took place.

The FBI did not ask the Russians for additional information.

The FBI did not put the two brothers under surveillance.

The FBI did not warn the Boston police.

In the end the multiple Russian warnings did not prevent the bombers from carrying out their atrocity.

There are still many questions about the Tsarnaev brothers, particularly how Tamerlan was not stopped by the No Fly list and why the US security services failed to pursue strong evidence provided by Russia's intelligence organizations.

Like the Tsarnaev case, the Manchester Arena bomber was well known to British police and intelligence.

The bomber and his father had fought in Libya on behalf of Islamic Jihadist organizations, and the bomber himself may have received additional training in Syria, perhaps by Hezbollah (a terrorist organization sponsored by

Iran). The British had rescued the father and son from Libya, because both were British citizens. But, again the authorities failed to do their job, insisting that the bomber, Salman Ramadan Abedi was not a high-level threat.

The Manchester bomber case raises many questions that remain unanswered including why the British authorities downplayed any threat from Salman Abedi or why they were "rescued" from Libya when many others were not.

In April, 2017 a Coptic Christian church was bombed in the city of Tanta, north of Cairo, as worshipers were celebrating Palm Sunday. At least 25 people were killed and more than 60 were injured.

In January, 2019 bombs went off during Sunday mass at a Philippine Catholic cathedral in the mostly Muslim autonomous region called Muslim Mindanao.

Two explosions inside and outside of Our Lady of Mt. Carmel Cathedral killed more than 20 people and wounded dozens on January 27 in Sulu province in the south of Mindanao.

In all these cases there had been plenty of prior warnings.

It is sometimes the case that intelligence and law enforcement organizations fail to grasp the seriousness of a threat. But it may also be true that at least some of these individuals were playing a dual role and providing "useful" intelligence, giving them a kind of protective status. It may take years to find out the truth, and some of the doubts and questions may never be answered. The consequence of both is that those concerned with security have to prepare and organize properly and not take assurance for granted.

Firebombing

Firebombing has also been used to destroy churches. Three black churches were intentionally set ablaze in St. Landry Parish, Louisiana, over the course of ten days in late March and early April, 2019.

On the 16th of April, 2019 firefighters in Needham, Massachusetts, about 20 miles from Boston, responded to reports of a fire at the Chabad Jewish Center.

Thirty minutes away in Arlington, police and firefighters had responded to reports of a fire at Rabbi Avi Burkiet's home, which also functions as a community Chabad Center. Luckily, these fires did not result in major damage.

On April 19, 2019 several incendiary devices were found on the perimeter of Chicago's north-side Anshe Shalom synagogue. Its rabbi, David Wolkenfeld, said that the devices did no damage to the building locating on Melrose Street near Lakeshore Drive. The synagogue is in a residential area and sits next to a Jewish Community Center. The police and FBI reviewed video camera recordings that showed that a man entered the synagogue parking lot shortly after midnight and tried to set the building on fire using an incendiary device.

One of the common devices used in firebombing is called, derisively, the Molotov cocktail. It is a petrol/gasoline device that typically is a small mouthed bottle filled with gasoline with a gasoline-soaked rag stuffed into its opening. The rag is ignited and the "cocktail" is thrown at or dropped on the target.

The original Molotov cocktail. (Ohto Kokko [CC BY-SA 3.0])
The Finns gave this sort of petrol bomb its infamous name during the Russo-Finnish war in 1939.

In an attack on a church, synagogue, mosque, temple or religiously-based community center, a typical scenario might be to throw rocks through glass windows and then toss a Molotov cocktail into the building.

Such a petrol bomb can do a lot of damage.

In 2018 a synagogue in Houston, Texas, an Orthodox congregation called Torah Vachesed (Torah Piety) Synagogue, may have been hit by a petrol bomb. Congregants said they heard an explosion and then a fire broke out. Local firefighters were able to rescue the synagogue's Torah scrolls, although two had some water damage. Congregants were in the building at the time in an evening study session.

In May, 2017 a three-alarm fire broke out at the Beth Hamedrash Hagadol (Great Study House) Synagogue, causing serious damage. What caused the fire has not been determined. (On October 23, 2019 the burnt synagogue was being taken down to be replaced by a commercial complex. A construction worker was killed by a structural collapse.)

A mosque was firebombed in Escondido, California in March, 2019. The Dar-ul-Arqam (Arqam ibn Abi'l-Arqam c. 597-675, was a companion of Muhammad) Mosque sustained damage to the exterior of the building. News reports say that the mosque's security camera spotted an unidentifiable person breaking a lock to a parking lot gate and then pouring a flammable liquid near a side door and setting it on fire.

A New Haven, Connecticut, Diyanet Center of America Mosque was firebombed on May 13, 2019. The mosque is a Turkish-American mosque. The attack took place during the Ramadan holiday period. It would appear an incendiary device (probably a petrol bomb) was thrown through a window above the rear door of the mosque.

There are many more reports of arson against churches, mosques, synagogues, temples and community centers.

These types of attacks are difficult to prevent because the perimeter of most buildings are not protected and often lack motion sensors, cameras and other security systems, such as good illumination. Many buildings feature glass windows and doors that can easily be shattered.

Among the defenses against fire bombs are motion and breakage sensors connected to alarms, good surveillance camera systems, patrolling guards, and "hardening" of near ground level windows using Plexiglas or other unbreakable cladding material. Also helpful are automatic fire extinguishers near windows and doors and on rooftops, because a fire starting on a roof can cause substantial damage, such as the massive fire that engulfed Notre Dame Cathedral in Paris. It also goes without saying that smoke detectors including carbon monoxide sensors should be placed throughout buildings, including attic and storage areas.

Stabbings

There have been numerous stabbings outside and inside church properties in the United States and abroad.

In Rockville, Maryland a son stabbed his mother to death outside a Roman Catholic Church.

A woman was stabbed outside a Canal street church in New Orleans. New Orleans police arrested Uhuru Howard, a 46-year-old woman who was also suspected of a separate stabbing in January. These stabbings occurred as parents were dropping off children at a day care center, which is part of the church.

In Texas, at a home worship service, a 61-year-old man died of his injuries, while the church's 54-year-old pastor was hospitalized after 28-year-old Marco Antonio Moreno stabbed them both and then surrendered to other congregants.

Police reported that Moreno had an alcohol- and drug-related history.

In January, 2019 a 24-year-old Scientologist was stabbed in the neck with a large kitchen knife by a teenager he was escorting off the church premises in Sydney, Australia.

In 2015, in Frederick, Maryland a homeless Virginia man fatally stabbed a South Korean missionary and seriously wounded his wife at a church retreat center.

In April, 2019 Daniel Jay Porter, 34, stabbed 41-year-old Shadab A. Siddiqi, in the chest with a steak knife during an argument between the two that took place inside the Annoor Mosque in Knoxville, Tennessee.

A German citizen of Afghan background stabbed an Orthodox rabbi in Frankfurt. A 22-year-old man was arrested after the attack on Rabbi Zalman Gurevitch and charged with attempted murder and causing a life-threatening injury. Gurevitch was stabbed in the stomach on his way home from Shabbat (Sabbath) services.

A rabbi and two of his congregants were stabbed in 2015, outside a synagogue in Marseilles, France. Police arrested the assailant, who shouted antisemitic epithets at the victims and reportedly was drunk at the time of the attack. According to Le Figaro, the assailant was known to local police and was considered mentally unstable.

Stabbings have increased, especially after Middle Eastern terrorists have used knives and swords to commit various crimes, from ISIS-led beheadings to Palestinians stabbing Israeli citizens. The knife phenomena has spread abroad, especially to Western Europe, where such attacks have multiplied. In the UK there is a veritable epidemic of knife attacks, often by local thugs and teenage gangs.

It is not surprising that attacks in holy places using knives seem to be on the upswing. Some of the church-related incidents involve domestic conflicts or mental illness, others are racially or ideologically motivated. It doesn't matter much to the victims what lies behind the threat.

The reality is that knives are easy to conceal. Few congregations have metal detectors, so spotting a concealed knife is very difficult and discovery is unlikely. Even at sites where packages are checked, a knife can still be smuggled in clothing, such as heavy overcoats.

On October 3, 2019 an employee of the Paris Police at the station on the Ile de la Cite killed four co-workers in a frenzied knife attack. The killer, Michael Harpon, had been employed by the police for some twenty years as a computer expert, but had converted to Islam and apparently joined a radical Salafist Islamic Movement. Harpon used a 13 inch ceramic knife. The ceramic knife was selected because it is not picked up by metal detectors.

There were metal detectors at the Police headquarters. However, there were no bag checks.

IMPORTANT: One of the best indicators of a threat, whether it is a gun, a knife or a concealed bomb is when an individual is inappropriately dressed for the season, such as a heavy jacket or coat in warm weather.

Alert guards at airports, train stations and at houses of worship often can spot people behaving strangely, dressed inappropriately, who are unfamiliar, and who may be carrying a weapon.

The problem is trickier when the dress of a visitor may conform to certain religious dress standards. For example, a person dressed as a nun, as a religious Moslem woman (wearing a Hijab), or as an Orthodox Jew (heavy, black frock coat) often can fool even the best observers.

The Jewish Press reports[22] that in June, 2019, "A terrorist armed with three knives attempted to enter two synagogues in the Belgian city of Antwerp during the two-day Jewish holiday of Shavuot (Pentecost), but was stopped by alert security guards both times.

"The terrorist, a man reportedly of Iraqi descent, pretended to be Jewish, wearing a yarmulke (skull cap)."

In Tel Aviv, at the Sarona Market, two terrorists from the West Bank town of Hebron were dressed as Orthodox Jews. They killed four people at the Sbarro® restaurant in the market. CNN initially misreported them as Orthodox Jewish gunmen.

There are many different disguises used by criminals, ranging from clown costumes to beards and wigs, as well as cross dressing and even coloring skin to appear as a different racial type.

What We Can Learn?

People who want to deal violence have many options, whether by shooting, bombing, stabbing and all the many variations available to them.

It is clear that there are a variety of different motivations of individuals and group-organized and led attacks on religious institutions.

To name a few: White Supremacists, Radical Islamists, Antisemites, Anti-Hindus, Anti-Muslims, Anti-Catholics, Anti-Christians, Racists and much more. There are also gender issues, people who feel they are bullied or mistreated, and all sorts of mental health issues. There are workplace grudges and violence. There are family arguments that get out of control. There are criminals who don't respect the sanctity of a religious place and will carry out a violent act there as well as anyplace else.

The main point to understand is that a religious place is a vulnerable place unless it is protected. Because it is the focus not only of prayer, but also of social justice, a religious place comes into focus for haters as an opportunistic target.

It is important to keep in mind that a violent attack can take many forms and a good security system is needed to detect and interdict a threat before an attack can fully materialize.

IMPORTANT: Remember that the softer the target (that is, the less it has security protection) the more likely it will be attacked. If the target is hard –that is, well protected, and the protection is strong and visible, there is a better chance that an armed and violent person will be deterred.

CHAPTER 3

Basic Security Concepts

Why Run, Hide, Fight is a Poor Security Model

The FBI Run, Hide, Fight model, endorsed by many security professionals in the United States and abroad, proposes that in the case of an Active Shooter those impacted should first run, then if that fails hide, and if, and only if that fails, fight.

The FBI has promoted this model extensively. Unfortunately, it has been misunderstood and many organizations, including religious ones have used it to design how they might respond in the case of an active shooter. Sometimes by adopting this model community leaders have mistaken the forest for the trees: they have used this as the only guidepost needed to deal with a crisis. While the model is not virtue-less, it is in its essence a defeatist paradigm because it leads organizations of all kinds to think this is the planning approach they should take.

The model was put clearly to the test in the Pittsburgh Tree of Life Synagogue Active Shooter incident where some congregants hid inside a closet downstairs from the main temple. The shooter found them and killed them all. In consequence of the shooting, Tree of Life Synagogue closed its doors in 2019.

Memorials to the Dead at Pittsburgh's Tree of Life Synagogue
(Official White House Photo by Andrea Hanks)

The fight scenario was again tested at the University of North Carolina, where Riley Howell, 21, was killed when he physically attacked the shooter. His action no doubt helped save lives, but the cost was his own life.

Similarly, Liviu Librescu, who was a Romanian–American scientist and engineer at Virginia Tech was killed on April 16, 2007 holding shut classroom doors, enabling other students to flee. He died from gunshot wounds.

The Run, Hide, Fight model assumes that a venue has been completely penetrated by an Active Shooter. In many of the video and slide presentations shown by the FBI and passed down to police departments around the USA and elsewhere, the presentation focuses on people diving under desks or running away from a shooter. Typically, "fight" is not shown or addressed because an Active Shooter's targets are usually not armed.

As Mike Wood[23], a tactical expert has written: "The [FBI] film and [Run, Hide, Fight] model encourage a 'soft' response to violence, preconditioning the victim to escape or hide as the preferred means of survival…. Potential victims are taught that the risks associated with fighting an attacker are much greater than the risk from running away, so violence can only be used 'as a last resort' when all other options have been tried, and failed."

The Freeze Problem

Wood goes on to talk about the problem of "freeze" which is that humans "confronted with sudden and unexpected violence" freeze unless they are trained otherwise.

Freeze leads to panic or worse, panic induced paralysis, and victims are left completely unprepared for the reality of the attack.

Relying on Run, Hide, and Fight also conditions staff and its leadership to have the same mental state as victims, unless thoroughly trained otherwise. The Run, Hide, Fight approach does not directly address training or the overall psychological impact of an Active Shooter incident.

In "real life" Active Shooter Incidents there are only a few cases of "fight" (and then only by armed guards) and the scenario to "run and hide" has come up short and failed to save lives. This has been observed particularly in indoor and outdoor theatre settings, in nightclubs, in meeting halls and in churches, mosques, temples and synagogues where the victims are often in a theatre-like setting. In all these examples there have been many victims.

- A proper plan needs to focus on what happens *before* the police arrive. The objective is to prevent or delay an active shooter from penetrating a venue.
- Strategies need to be implemented to find ways to block an active shooter giving time for police to arrive while minimizing casualties.

In these situations, the police will almost certainly need the support of staff and in-house security in order to neutralize the shooter and minimize "friendly fire" incidents.

IMPORTANT: Staff need to assist the police in locating the shooter, understanding where the shooter might escape or hide, and support the police to operate in as secure a mode as possible (e.g., avoid police casualties).

The Critical 5 Minutes

A workable and effective Security Plan must account for the 5 minutes before police and emergency personnel can arrive on the scene, keeping in mind that the "5 minutes" could in reality take longer because police may have to be summoned from other operations and not only from their headquarters, have to deal with traffic and congestion on the streets, and will need to take time to understand where the threat is before attempting neutralization.

On some occasions, police may not act until they get additional reinforcements or specialized counter-terror SWAT teams.

The 5-minute period should not be squandered. Along with calling 911, there are a number of intermediate steps to help avoid or minimize casualties.

What this means in practice is that every effort should be made to block an active shooter for as long as possible.

Active Shooter Methodology

From what has been learned of Active Shooters, the shooter (or shooters) will often pre-plan the attack, trying to understand their chance to penetrate a facility.

IMPORTANT: Most of the incidents that are known involve settings where the level of perimeter/site security was poor or only one or two guards at most blocked a successful penetration.

The Shooter will try and see if his entrance with a weapon will be blocked. There are a number of scenarios, but the most common ones are:

Push into premises with guns blazing.

This is what happened at the Bataclan Club in Paris and also at the Holocaust Museum in Washington, DC.

Civil Service of Remembrance in Paris (photo by Mstyslav Chernov, Wikipedia Commons)

At about 12:50 p.m. on June 10, 2009, 88-year old white supremacist James Wenneker von Brunn entered the United States Holocaust Memorial Museum in Washington, D.C. with a rifle and fatally shot Museum Special Police Officer Stephen Tyrone Johns. Other security guards returned fire, wounding von Brunn, who was then apprehended. In this case an armed guard was shot, but the Shooter was himself wounded and apprehended by other guards.

In some locales, armed guards are posted both outside and inside buildings to prevent a "push" type assault.

In Israel many restaurants hire armed, security guards, inspect bags and take other measures to prevent shootings from outside (e.g., shooting through large glass windows).

In the Push scenario, there is very little time, but to the degree that the main hall and entrance can be locked down, the Shooter can be partly contained. The ability to lock down is governed by many factors, including the layout of the facility and the control over entrances.

In cases where the Security Staff is not armed, the Shooter's access can be partially limited by technological means such as magnetic locking doors that can be activated before the Shooter penetrates a facility, very loud alarms to attempt to frighten the shooter away, and the use of non-lethal, immobilizing technology including Tasers, "wrap" technology (such as the BolaWrap®100 restraint device), immobilizing sprays, rubber bullets etc. In the case of large glass exposure, the use of bullet-resistant glass is recommended.

IMPORTANT: Relying on less than lethal technology to stop an armed shooter is very risky and is not recommended. An armed shooter or shooters always have an advantage and the guard or volunteer attempting to use a less than lethal system is in dire danger.

Smuggle a weapon into a facility.

Carrying a weapons (gun, rifle, knife, or explosive device) into a building is very common, although most of the cases we know of have occurred where there was neither a security presence (or the security presence was limited and poorly trained), nor was there any inspection system in place to check bags, packages and equipment.

On December 2, 2015 14 people were killed and 22 others were seriously injured in a terrorist attack consisting of a mass shooting and an attempted bombing at the Inland Regional Center in San Bernardino, California. The Active Shooter perpetrators, Syed Rizwan Farook and Tashfeen Malik, a married couple living in the city of Redlands, targeted a San Bernardino County Department of Public Health training event and Christmas party of about 80 employees in a rented banquet room.

At 10:58 a.m., Farook and Malik, armed with semi-automatic pistols and rifles, fired five shots, killing two people outside the building. Farook then entered a minute later and opened fire on those in attendance, followed quickly by Malik. They wore ski masks and black, tactical gear, but no ballistic or bulletproof vests.

The entire shooting took two or three minutes, during which the shooters fired more than 100 bullets before fleeing. There were no security guards.

Farook had earlier been at the event as a participant, so he knew the set up and was able to use that information to carry out the attack. When he first left midway through the party, he put a backpack on a table filled with explosives. (The two shooters were later killed by the FBI and Police when their SUV was shot up by law enforcement. The backpack did not explode and was neutralized.)

San Bernardino shooters killed (By San Bernardino County Sheriff's Department, Public Domain)

In Aurora, Colorado at the Century 16 Movie Theatre an Active Shooting took place during a midnight viewing of the film "Dark Knight Rises." The shooter, James Eagan was able to enter the theatre with multiple firearms. There was no security present. Twelve people were killed and seventy others were injured, 58 of them from gunfire. The Shooter was arrested outside the theatre near his car. His apartment was also rigged with explosives and the police narrowly avoided another serious incident.

Enter the enclosed area or gain shooting access from an unlocked exit, loading dock or parking lot.

This most famous incident occurred in Las Vegas on October 1, 2017, when a gunman opened fire on a crowd of concertgoers at the Route 91 Harvest music festival.

The shooter shot from the 32nd floor of the adjacent Mandalay Bay Hotel. He smuggled weapons, weapons stands, electronics and other gear to a room he rented, using the hotel underground parking lot, and carrying the hardware on a freight elevator.

While the smuggling of his weapons was caught on surveillance video, none of the security personnel in the Hotel apparently took notice or discovered that an unauthorized person was using the freight elevator numerous times.

In the incident, the Shooter was able to train his weapons on the outdoor crowd for around 10 minutes; it would be a full hour before the shooting location was identified and neutralized. Some 58 people were killed and 851 injured, over 400 of them by gunfire and hundreds more in the ensuing panic.

The Shooter was able to pick off his victims at will and kill or wound them when they tried to escape. Run and Hide was of no value in this incident and there was no possibility of Fight.

Drive-by Shooting or related vehicle incident.

Drive-by shootings are increasingly common and can be related to some perceived hatred, can be linked to terrorism or other organized hate group, can be carried out by someone who is mentally unstable, or be aimed at a group or class of people or at a specific individual. In some cases, the shooter will wound or kill a completely innocent bystander. In one case in the District of Columbia, a small child who was indoors died when a stray bullet fired from a car smashed through the home's window and struck the child.

Vehicles may also be used to bring death and destruction. In 2017 in New York eight people were killed and more than a dozen injured when a man drove a truck down a bike path. His path of destruction covered nearly a mile in lower Manhattan, striking pedestrians, cyclists, joggers and a school bus.

On December 19, 2016, a truck was deliberately driven into the Christmas market next to the Kaiser Wilhelm Memorial Church at Breitscheidplatz in Berlin, leaving 12 people dead and 56 others injured. One of the victims was the truck's original driver, Łukasz Urban, who was found shot dead in the passenger seat.

On the evening of July 14, 2016, a 19-tonne cargo truck was deliberately driven into crowds of people celebrating Bastille Day on the Promenade des Anglais in Nice, France, resulting in the deaths of 86 people and the injury of 458 others. The driver was Mohamed Lahouaiej-Bouhlel, a Tunisian resident of France.

On July 28, 2019 a congregant of the Young Israel of Greater Miami synagogue was shot at least four times while waiting for evening services to start. The shooter apparently was in a vehicle driving by the synagogue. The motive isn't yet known and the shooter was not apprehended. The victim, Yosef Lifshutz, 68, was sitting on an outside bench when the drive-by shooting occurred. The victim survived.

Organizing to Deal with Active Shooter Threats

Operational Model

In order to mitigate or prevent Active Shooter attacks faith based institutions must be properly organized, apply the right strategies, have appropriate technology and have a well trained staff. At the heart of the matter is to have the right operational model; without it stopping a shooter may be impossible.

Instead of Run, Hide, or Fight a proposed operational model aims to (1) identify; (2) intercept; (3) isolate and (4) protect.

- **Identify** means the ability to rapidly identify a potential Shooter
- **Intercept** means to attempt to stop or block a shooter before full penetration of a venue

- **Isolate** means to divert a Shooter wherever possible away from crowds or entrances
- **Protect** means to employ effective means to protect as many people as possible from an Active Shooter

---

This is the Operational Model. Not all elements of the Model will be available to every security staff. But the security staff must be trained to use these methods as the most effective means of limiting potential harm to individuals.

The FBI should update its Run, Hide, Fight security model to <u>Identify, Intercept, Isolate and Protect</u> because Run, Hide, Fight has failed to save lives in practice and because it is a poor model for designing security systems.

Places where there is any danger of any attack should have a trained security staff who understand what they need to do to confront an active shooter. Correlated with the security staff, useful technology to inhibit an entering shooter, protect employees and visitors and thwart a shooter until reinforced police units arrive is a better security model which the FBI should embrace.

Important Lessons

- The purpose of any Security Plan is to Protect and Save lives
- The Plan should be proactive and not passive
- The Plan should be in effect and act **as a deterrent** before police arrive in case of an active shooter or stabbing incident
- The Plan should only rely on run or flee when an evacuation or escape from a shooter or other intruder is a practical alternative –in this case evacuation procedures should be carefully designed and staff and congregation trained appropriate
- A proactive Security Plan needs careful organization and preparation as most attackers go after soft targets, that is where there isn't a strong organization and presence of security personnel and systems
- Understand that an attack will not come "out of the blue" –in most cases, attacks are planned in advance and security preparations (if any) will be tested –it is important to look for signs and signals that someone or some group is planning an assault. These indicators can be found by noticing the presence of unknown or suspicious vehicles or persons lurking around a holy place, hostile telephone calls or messages, unexpected visitors or persons asking sensitive questions about security and safety, unknown individuals especially those with cameras, or who are circling around a facility, whether on foot, on bicycles or scooters, or in vehicles
- Keep in mind that an attacker will be well armed including semi-automatic weapons and in many cases will have practiced using those weapons to improve proficiency
- Deception is in the toolbox of many active shooters and bombers and they will employ many tricks to fool unsuspecting congregants, such as dressing like them, showing up with a "sob story" about their personal problems, or a wide range of other means of gaining

access ("I am hungry," or "I need spiritual help" are among the more common)

- Relying only on early warning from local police or from other intelligence sources to prepare against an intruder is a mistake because many active shooters and bombers either are not on the "radar" of law enforcement, or when they are known to law enforcement or intelligence, they are not seen as a high-level threat. In addition law enforcement often can't legally provide hard information because of disclosure restrictions
- It is important to treat all threats seriously and to immediately report them to local police and make preparations for a security incident. Reporting alone will never be enough to protect lives or property
- It is perfectly reasonable to ask for police protection of important events or where there is a known threat, keeping in mind that almost everywhere law enforcement is overextended and overburdened, as well as short on personnel. It is definitely worth paying for extra protection

---

Religious institutions are a target for terrorists, haters and people who are mentally ill, whether recognized as such by the courts or not

Identifying a threat profile (active shooter, bomber etc.) is basic to being able to prepare a proper defense

Intercepting a threat can stop an incident before it happens

Isolating a threat, well away from the congregation is an important way to delay the threat until police can arrive at the scene

"Protecting" in the case of an active shooter means to have a capability on site to challenge an armed attacker. Without this capability the intruder can easily penetrate the heart of any religious institution and create havoc and carnage

CHAPTER 4

Perimeter Security

E very Security Plan has to work to protect both the outside as well as the inside of a religious site.

The outside area is very important. The key reasons to protect the outside are:

- To head off an active threat by identifying and intercepting the threat before he/she/they penetrates the interior of the religious site
- To deal with attacks that may be directed at congregants entering or leaving the holy place
- To protect against bombs that may be placed in or around the building
- To protect against incendiaries such as Molotov cocktails
- To safeguard parking areas
- To block any attack launched by a vehicle against the building or the congregants or both

---

There are of course different challenges that come from the location of the building, whether it is an urban, suburban or rural area, whether it is an isolated location, if there are major roadways near the building, whether it is a campus that includes a place of worship and a separate school, day care or senior center or areas that are used by the general community for activities ranging from Bingo games to fitness training.

There are also religiously-based organizations that operate in many cities and suburban areas. Groups like B'nai Brith, Catholic Charities USA, Bharat Sevashram Sangha of North America, the US Council of Muslim Organizations, Jewish Federations around the United States, religiously-based community centers, religious retreats, day camps and overnight camps, and many lobbying organizations supporting religious or religiously-linked causes.

Many hospitals also are closely associated with or affiliated with religious groups. One in six hospital patients[24] in the United States are now treated in a Catholic facility, according to the Catholic Health Association. Approximately 113 Jewish hospitals were founded in the history of the United States and that there are now about 22 left. Some of these, however are among the best in the United States. For example, Barnes-Jewish Hospital in St. Louis was ranked first in 10 data-driven specialties and received the highest rating in 9 common care procedures.

Some Catholic, Jewish, Adventist, Mormon, Methodist and other denominations have merged in recent years. For example, Beth Israel Hospital and New England Deaconess Hospital, a Methodist facility, merged in 1996.

There have been active shooter incidents in hospitals. At the Brigham and Women's hospital in Boston, a cardiac surgeon, Michael Davidson, who was director of endovascular cardiac was shot twice at the hospital's cardiovascular center. The gunman, identified as Stephen Pasceri, then shot himself. Both men died.

In 2017 at the Bronx-Lebanon hospital in New York, a shooter killed a doctor and wounded six people with an AR-15 semi-automatic rifle. The shooter was later identified as 45-year-old Nigerian-born Dr. Henry Michael Bello, a family physician formerly employed by the hospital.

In December, 2017 a gunman opened fire at the University of Cincinnati Medical Center's psychiatric services emergency room, injuring an unarmed security officer before fatally shooting himself.

In November, 2018 four individuals died in a shooting at Mercy Hospital & Medical Center in Chicago, including an emergency room physician, a first-year pharmacy resident, a police officer and the alleged gunman.

Very few religious organizations and institutions have sound security and most, in fact, do not have any security. While hospitals typically have registration desks for visitors, and sometimes guards at the front entrance, most of these are stopgap measures of questionable effectiveness. Perimeter security is typically lacking.

Before You Begin: Prepare a Diagram of the Building Exterior & Grounds

Before executing the steps below make sure you have a good, schematic diagram of the congregation's property that includes roadways and any other feature of importance (such as parking lots, nearby buildings etc.).

IMPORTANT: Always treat all diagrams (both interior and exterior) as confidential documents. Don't send them around by email or post diagrams on social media account or websites.

Next, carry out a walking survey.

Bring a camera or mobile phone with a camera and make photos of the perimeter.

All such photos also are confidential documents.

It is a good idea to number all entrances and exits. These numbers should be placed in plain view so in case of an emergency law enforcement can be directly to the proper entrance. The numbering system also should be reflected in surveillance cameras images to readily identify a location.

If there are CCTV cameras installed for security, identify their locations and approximate coverage and indicate that on the diagram. Check if the existing cameras can cover street and parking lot and whether the quality of the imagery is good enough to capture license plates on vehicles.

Make sure you note where windows are, especially for the sanctuary and chapel (if present), plus classrooms, meeting rooms, social halls etc. If the windows are at street level, consider whether they could be easily smashed or broken, and whether an intruder could gain access to the facility. Consideration should be given to reinforcing accessible windows (including bars) and breakage detectors should be installed and connected to an alarm system. Also make sure cameras cover all window areas.

Take note of the location of automobile parking in relation to the building and note any vulnerabilities. Is access to parking lots controlled and if so, how? Are there warning signs posted on parking lots? Is their good lighting in the parking lot? Does the parking lot have an emergency call box?

Mark out locations of fences and gates and make notes on the strength and utility of gates and fences. Can someone easily climb over the fence or barrier? Is there video coverage of the gates and fences? Are there any sensors along the fences? Can any gate or fence accessible from a roadway be broken down easily by a vehicle?

Make sure a vehicle cannot smash into vulnerable parts of the building, such as doorways and windows. Check to see if there are strong obstacles (such as boulders) or bollards to protect against vehicular attacks. Some congregations use large, decorative rocks or boulders that prevent any vehicle from crashing into a building or used to assault congregants. Bollards and other types of security barriers should be considered and installed by qualified engineers.

Mark the operating entrance clearly on the diagram. Mark other entrances or doorways and check whether they are usually locked or open. Check, too that the locking systems are strong and effective. Is there any monitoring of locked doors? Are the locked doors tied into the security system? Is the security system "live" during religious services, school activities, etc.? You may need an alarm specialist to help test the system and make needed adjustments or changes. Also a good engineer can test the integrity of the door locks or locking system.

Note locations of any security devices such as motion detectors, location of outside alarm boxes etc.

Check to see how well (if at all) pedestrians are protected from threats such as attacks launched from automobiles or trucks.

Make notes (preliminary) where volunteers and guards should be positioned. If possible, on a church day, see where guards are actually located (if present at all) and note that information on the diagram.

Google Maps

Check what is shown about the grounds and buildings on Google Maps. You may be surprised to find that quite a lot of information is available that could be used by an active shooter or bomber in planning an attack.

There is probably not much you can do about Google Maps observations of your property (which Google shows both a traditional street map and in the form of color satellite photos of the property and surroundings).

Of course, you can use Google Maps material to back up your working diagrams. But keep in mind that Google's satellite coverage may show photos that are a few years old while the actual maps are more recent.

Identify Nearest Police Station and Fire Department

The map you prepare should be supplemented with information on the location of the nearest police and fire departments.

Drive to and from those locations to gain an estimate of the time it would take to get assistance.

Identify nearby hospitals and clinics.

How long would it take to get an ambulance to your site? What is the time to respond for police, fire brigade and other emergency services? Put this information in your report and on the diagram.

Know Your Police & First Responders

- Congregational leaders and ministers, priests, rabbis and imams and temple leaders, ordained and lay, should visit with local police and firefighters and invite them to reciprocate the visit by coming to look over the premises of the congregation (and affiliated places such as religious schools, day care centers, senior centers, etc.). These relationships are all important and should not ever be neglected.
- In many areas police and firefighters, and first responders are willing to make suggestions and even to brief congregational leadership on how best they can provide help.
- Having the police and fire fighters keep a diagram of your building will be of inestimable help in case of an incident.

Evacuation Areas

Locating exit doors (especially from the sanctuary, social hall and classrooms) and where to direct evacuees in case of an emergency should be evaluated on a preliminary basis in the initial walk around.

Exits should be marked and congregants instructed in where they need to go in case of an incident. Plainly mark exit routes and practice using them.

IMPORTANT: Is there a nearby facility (another church, recreation center, public building) that is likely to be accessible on a church day to take in evacuees? This is important, because police and other emergency personnel will be arriving on the scene and need space to operate, and an accounting of people who were evacuated safely will be urgently needed. For their investigation the police will also need to interview eye witnesses.

Estimate the walking time from the exit doors to the site where evacuees should reassemble. Consider if there are steps or other obstacles that could hinder an evacuation.

Volunteers, staff and church officials need to be aware of designated evacuation areas.

ELDERLY AND CHILDREN

- Remember there are elderly and infirm people in every congregation. They should not be left behind, and plans should be made to help them in case of any evacuation (whether for security or safety reasons). Wheel chairs, stretchers or other equipment should be on hand in addition to medical emergency supplies. It is not uncommon for people to have adverse physical reactions in stressful situations including hyperventilating, uncontrolled shaking or vomiting, heart palpitations and heart attacks or aberrant behaviour. Seek appropriate training for staff to handle these situations.
- Very often children are separated from parents, for example in nurseries or classrooms during religious services. In an emergency parents will want to go to their children, which may not be possible. Staff and leadership need to be aware and factor this into their emergency planning.

First Step–Identifying Places of Maximum Vulnerability

Weak or non-existent perimeter protection provides many opportunities for an attacker.

The obvious most important step is to protect the entrance or entrances, and make it difficult for a subject to approach the entrance of the building with visible weapons.

Entrances are not the only point of vulnerability, but if the entrance permits easy access to the facility, it rates very high on the list of major concerns.

Most physical attackers (other than in some bombings) generally assault the easiest access point, and this is usually the main entrance.

Consider, for example, the Poway Synagogue where the attacker just walked in because the door was open and unguarded.

Exactly the same thing happened in Pittsburgh at the Tree of Life Synagogue. And the same happened at the Sutherland Springs First Baptist Church.

In all these cases there were warnings of one kind or another, indeed rather specific warnings in the case of Pittsburgh, but entrances were left unlocked and unguarded.

TAKE NOTE: Some congregations are not using the large, main entrance of their place of worship. This is because these entrances often are vulnerable and very hard to protect. For example many classic churches main doors open immediately to the sanctuary, leaving no space to control a threat. For this reason, access is diverted to a well manned and protected side entrance.

Use of Guards, Armed and Unarmed

There are many different entrance control strategies.

All of them begin with having a guard or guards at the entrance.

A guard should be considered the minimal first step.

While a guard is a deterrent, if the guard is unarmed or is elderly or is just a volunteer from the congregation, the likelihood of actually stopping determined intruders is not very good. If the guard is wearing street clothes and no uniform, no protective gear and has no obvious weapon, the guard will not provide much deterrent for the congregation and neither the police nor congregants will know the person is a guard.

There is an active debate about whether guards at religious organizations and institutions should be armed.

Usually those against armed guards are also against having any guards at all, which they see as intruding on the welcoming nature of the faith or confession.

But assuming that the "compromise" is to have an unarmed guard or guards, congregants should ask themselves if an unarmed guard is an ethical alternative.

An unarmed guard is most likely to be hurt, shot or killed by an armed intruder. Even if the guard is wearing a protective vest (bulletproof vest), he or she can still suffer a serious life-threatening injury or death.

It is important to keep in mind that a guard is being asked to put his or her life in front of the congregation's lives. That is a non-trivial "ask" and it has to be tempered by taking full responsibility for all the consequences. Responsibility is not just a legal or contractual issue, it is a human issue of considerable consequence.

In some jurisdictions, armed guards are not allowed because of national or local laws. This is more common outside the United States.

In the UK, most places that need armed guards are guarded with either military or police. Security guards in the UK cannot carry guns, with the exception being protection of certain politicians and defense installations, including some defense companies. According to the London Metropolitan Police a "rape siren" is the only mechanical deterrent a civilian can carry. You may not carry; a firearm, knife, chemical spray, baton, club, brass knuckles, etc.

Italy supplies thousands of armed, security guards, mainly soldiers and Carabinieri (state police) at tourist centers, synagogues and other potential terrorist targets. Private security personnel guarding banks, shopping malls and other facilities (in recent years, even some public offices and hospitals in Italy have contracted private security personnel for 24/7 protection) are allowed to carry guns.

One company in Germany[25] that provides security services has a corporate security gun license. Pond Security Group guards carry guns and the company can rapidly place armed guards throughout Germany as needed. At the time of this writing, Pond Security is the only security company with such a license in Germany.

Unlike the US, in Europe it is possible to have government-supplied guards where there is a perceived threat. But because of tough gun laws and, dwindling church membership, and limited ability to provide coverage, most churches in Europe are without protection. In the United States local police can provide physical protection (sometimes charging for the service), but availability is an issue.

Most armed guards in Europe wear appropriate combat gear, meaning they wear SWAT-type helmets, protective vests and carry with them police-type tactical radios and (sometimes) body-cams. Weapons include handguns, assault rifles and shotguns. Police may also carry stun and flash grenades, Tasers and disabling agents.

For armed guards at churches, mosques, temples and synagogues, semi-automatic hand guns plus protective vests are appropriate along with radio communications gear. Kevlar®-type Helmets[26] are strongly recommended.

There are many semi-automatic handguns. Here is a list[27] of some of the more common, many of which are known to have been used by active shooters:

- Colt 1911 government model 7+1 shot .45
- CZ (ČZUB) 75.
- Browning Hi-Power 13+1 shot
- 9 mm Luger pistol.
- Glock 17 Gen 4 17+1 shot
- Smith & Wesson double-action .45
- ACP semi-automatic compact pistol.
- M9 pistol used by the US military; a variant of the Beretta 92FS.

There are many semi-automatic rifles in the marketplace, and there are kits and information on how they can be modified to turn them into fully automatic weapons (capable of continuously firing by holding the trigger back).

One common addition is known as the Bump Stock[28], which the Trump administration made illegal in the United States. But there are still thousands of bump stocks in the hands of gun owners. The Las Vegas shooter[29], Stephen Paddock, had bump stocks on twelve of his semi-automatic rifles recovered after the horrific shooting of outdoor concert goers.

Here is a full list of Stephen Paddock's guns and equipment found at the hotel where the shooting happened and at other locations. The list is provided by the Las Vegas Police Department:

Guns found inside Mandalay Bay rooms 32-135 and 32-134:

- Colt M4 Carbine AR-15 .223/5.56 with a bump stock, vertical fore grip and 100 round magazine. Front sight only.
- Noveske N4 AR-15 .223/5.56 with a bump stock, vertical fore grip and 40 round magazine. EOTech optic.
- LWRC M61C AR-15 .223/5.56 with a bump stock, vertical fore grip and 100 round magazine. No sights or optics.
- POF USA P-308 AR-10 .308/7.62 with a bipod, scope and 25 round magazine
- Christensen Arms CA-15 AR-15 .223 Wylde with a bump stock, vertical fore grip and 100 round magazine. No sights or optics.
- POF USA P-15 P AR-15 .223/5.56 with a bump stock, vertical fore grip and 100 round magazine. No sights or optics.
- Colt Competition AR-15 .223/5.56 with a bump stock, vertical fore grip and 100 round magazine. No sights or optics.
- Smith & Wesson 342 AirLite .38 caliber revolver with 4 cartridges, 1 expended cartridge case.
- LWRC M61C AR-15 .223/5.56 with a bump stock, vertical fore grip and 100 round magazine. EOTech optic.
- FNH FM15 AR-10 .308/7.62 with a bipod, scope and 25 round magazine.

- Daniel Defense DD5V1 AR-10 .308/7.62 with a bipod, scope and 25 round magazine.
- FNH FN15 AR-15 .223/5.56 with a bump stock, vertical fore grip and 100 round magazine. EOTech optic.
- POF USA P15 AR-15 .223/5.56 with a bump stock, vertical fore grip and 100 round magazine. EOTech optic.
- Colt M4 Carbine AR-15 .223/5.56 with a bump stock, vertical fore grip and 100 round magazine.
- Daniel Defense M4A1 AR-15 .223/5.56 with a bump stock, vertical fore grip and 100 round magazine. EOTech optic.
- LMT Def. 2000 AR-15 .223/5.56 with a bump stock, vertical fore grip and 100 round magazine. No sights or optics.
- Daniel Defense DDM4V11 AR-15 .223/5.56 with a bump stock, vertical fore grip. No magazine. EOTech optic.
- Sig Sauer SIG716 AR-10 .308/7.62 with a bipod, red dot optic and 25 round magazine.
- Daniel Defense DD5V1 AR-10 .308/7.62 with a bipod and scope. No magazine.
- FNH FN15 AR-15 .223/5.56 with a bump stock, vertical fore grip and 100 round magazine. No sights or optics.
- Ruger American .308 caliber bolt action rifle with scope.
- LMT LM308MWS AR-10 .308/7.62 with a bipod and red dot scope. No magazine.
- Ruger SR0762 AR-10 .308/7.62 with a bipod, scope and 25 round magazine.
- LMT LM308MWS AR-10 with a bipod, scope and 25 round magazine.
- Guns found inside Paddock's Mesquite home:
- Smith & Wesson SW99 9mm semi-automatic pistol.
- Smith & Wesson M&P9 9mm semi-automatic pistol.
- Glock 17 9mm semi-automatic pistol.
- Mossberg 500 12 gauge pump action shotgun.
- Sig Sauer 516 AR-15 .223/5.56 rifle with a bipod and scope.
- Arma-Lite SPRM001 AR-15 .223/5.56 rifle with a bipod and scope.

- Mossberg 590 12 gauge pump action shotgun.
- LWRC M61C-IC-A5 AR-15 .223/5.56 rifle with a bipod and scope.
- Mossberg 590 V0348193 12 gauge pump action shotgun.
- Mossberg 930 12 semi-automatic gauge shotgun.
- Arma-Lite SPRM001 AR-15 .223/5.56 rifle with a bipod and scope.
- Sig Sauer 516 2AR-15 .223/5.56 rifle, with a bipod. No sights or optics.
- Lantac LA-R15 Raven AR-15 .223 Wylde rifle with a bipod and scope.
- Mossberg 590 12 gauge pump action shotgun.
- Arsenal Saiga 12 AK-47 style semi-automatic 12 gauge shotgun.
- Arsenal Saiga 12 AK-47 style semi-automatic 12 gauge shotgun.
- Beretta 92F 9mm semi-automatic pistol.
- FN 5.7 5.7mm semi-automatic pistol.

Guns found inside Paddock's Reno home:
- Smith & Wesson 340 .357 caliber revolver.
- Beretta Pietro 92A1 9 mm semi-automatic pistol.
- Remington Arms 870 Tactical 12 gauge pump action shotgun.
- Mossberg 590 12 gauge pump action shotgun.
- Glock 17 Gen4 9 mm semi-automatic pistol.
- Smith & Wesson M&P9 9 mm semi-automatic pistol.

Other evidence found inside Paddock's rooms at Mandalay Bay:
- Metal "L" bracket with three screws securing it to the interior door/frame.
- Two surveillance cameras from room service cart outside room 32-134.
- Bullet fragments
- Blue plastic hose with funnel, fan and SCUBA mouthpiece attached
- Surveillance camera mounted to room door peephole
- Baby monitor camera (not mounted). Surveillance camera mounted to room door peephole
- Small sledgehammer

- Laptop computer
- Surveillance camera monitor
- Spotting scope
- Binoculars
- Expended .223/5.56 cartridge casings (approximately 1,050)
- Cellular phones
- Nevada Driver's License – Stephen Paddock
- M life players card
- Polymer 40 round AR-15 magazines (loaded)
- Steel 100 round AR-15 magazines (loaded)
- Polymer 25 round AR-10 magazines (loaded). Live Ammunition (approximately 5,280)
- Handwritten note with distance/bullet drop calculations
- Suitcases
- Duffel bags
- Soft rifle cases
- Towels
- Laptop computer (on bed)
- Disassembled laptop computer missing hard drive (on floor)
- Power hand drills
- Empty ammunition boxes and plastic bags
- Scuba mask
- Loose ammunition
- Miscellaneous hand tools and drill bits
- Miscellaneous screws and mounting brackets
- Suitcases, towels
- Empty rifle magazines
- Laptop computer connected to hallway surveillance cameras
- Polymer 25 round AR-10 magazines (loaded)
- Expended .308/7.62 cartridge casings (8)
- 2017 Chrysler Pacifica, Nevada/74D401 towed to FBI garage
- 20x2 pound containers of exploding targets
- 10x1 pound containers of exploding targets

- 2x20 pound bags of explosive precursors
- Polymer 25 round AR-10 .308/7.62 magazines (loaded)
- Polymer 40 round AR-15 .223/5.56 magazines (loaded)
- Boxed ammunition
- Suitcases, towels

Despite the bump stock ban, bump stocks are still circulating and some are being smuggled in from as far away as China[30].

A Houston man, Ajay Dhingra was indicted[31] on September 5th, 2019 for firearms violations, possession "of a machine gun, [and] specifically a bump stock." It was also discovered that Dhingra allegedly made false statements in order to buy some of his firearms which he was prohibited from having because of mental illness issues in his past. In this case the weakness in gun control laws in not auditing or investigating claims about mental health (or declarations that the individual does not have a mental health issue), along with illegal possession of banned weapons demonstrates the gaps in US laws and regulations for gun control.

Catholic churches in France, synagogues in the UK and other organizations complement the armed guard services with volunteers, sometimes called "watchers" or in the Hebrew language, Shomrim.

The Briarwood Presbyterian Church[32] in Birmingham, Alabama, has created its own police force to protect its more than 4,000 members and 2,000 students and teachers.

Volunteers at Briarwood usually are unarmed, but may wear safety vests and carry radios that can communicate with the armed guards present at the Church location and their radios are linked to the local police.

Volunteers can perform many functions that strengthen perimeter security.

To begin with, as they are often drawn from the congregation the volunteers know most of the "regulars" who attend religious services. For those that they don't know, they can ask visitors their purpose in attending services or meetings, and who they may know.

In some religious organizations, unaccompanied and un-friended visitors are not permitted. This is true especially in areas where antisemitism is prevalent. In Greece, where the Jewish population was decimated by the Nazis, and where, since then, strong anti-Jewish pressure has come from political groups on the right and left, many synagogues will not accept any visitors.

In the United States, many churches, mosques and synagogues lack a clear policy on (unknown) visitors. A few, for example, in some larger cities including New York, Los Angeles and Washington, DC require a picture ID, a package or bag inspection or in some cases a congregant-sponsor. But for most, checks are minimal and even religious schools are poorly guarded.

ADVICE ON ENTRANCES
- Perimeter security should begin at the front gate or access door area. Unless guards can be put in place at alternative entry points (such as a side door), congregants and others should only be able to enter through the main entrance or the designated entrance, or through special needs entrances that also are monitored.
- Close communications between volunteers and security guards is a very important enhancement to the opportunity to head off an incident.

Armed Volunteers?

Congregants in some churches, synagogues and mosques bring their guns with them when they attend religious services or events. Under US concealed carry rules, there is nothing to prevent them from doing so. States and some municipalities regulate concealed carry permits or licenses, which are not always easy to obtain. In the United States, the Federal government defers to state and local regulations except where Federal property is concerned.

Congregants are sometimes asked to bring their guns with them if they have concealed carry permits. This was done at the Poway Chabad Synagogue near San Diego. Jonathan Morales, an off-duty Border Patrol agent brought his weapon to prayer after being urged to do so by the Poway's rabbi.

Morales is credited with saving lives, although Morales did not fire his gun[33] inside the synagogue. Instead Morales and a fellow congregant, Army veteran Oscar Stewart, attempted to subdue the gunman after the gunman's firearm jammed. Morales later gave chase and fired on the shooter, hitting his car.

Should volunteers, who are on security or watch duties, be armed? Where volunteers are used, for the most part they are not armed and are trained not to confront a threat but to call for help from security guards or police.

Is there an argument for volunteers being armed? The strongest case for armed volunteers is deterrence. A would-be attacker would have to think twice about the risk of facing armed guards, even if they are volunteers.

But there are also risks that include the danger of collateral casualties in any shoot out.

There is, in addition, no way to assure that the volunteers are properly trained and authorized to perform police functions. In some jurisdictions they may not be permitted to perform such functions.

IMPORTANT: For those considering armed volunteers it is strongly recommended that the local police and law enforcement authorities are consulted and local laws fully understood.

Another problem is operational—are guards with guns to act individually or under a commander? While police and military individuals are part of a formal chain of command, volunteers are not used to operating in a chain of command and most are not schooled on when it is acceptable to use a firearm. Anyone thinking about arming volunteers has to understand the possibly negative consequences when doing so.

The better organized volunteers are, and the better volunteers are taught to "report in" on a regular basis, the better a volunteer effort will function.

Armed volunteers, if they are armed, typically carry "light" weapons, mainly handguns. Unfortunately, an active shooter often has a semi-automatic weapon including rifles and handguns. From what we know of many active shooter incidents, the shooters are either weapon's savvy or have trained with the weapons before using them to carry out a violent attack. A semiautomatic can "spray" rounds at a volunteer, and the results are generally predictable.

It is well to remember that at the Poway synagogue the shooter only stopped firing when his gun jammed, not because he intended to stop. He was using a semi-automatic AR-15.

In Copenhagen, at the Great Synagogue, a gunman fired two 7.65 mm rounds and seven 9 mm rounds, hitting Dan Uzan, a 37-year-old Jewish community member on security duty who was killed and the shooter wounded two Danish security officers present nearby. Uzan was not armed, but the security officers were. The gunman had the advantage and acted before the volunteer or the officers were able to react. (Uzan was not wearing a security vest.)

What is the lesson we can draw? Where armed volunteers are permitted, and where they are properly trained and protected (for example by security vests), they can provide both deterrence and protection on the perimeter, although their service is not without significant risks.

Unarmed volunteers act in coordination with armed guards and police: they are trained not to engage a shooter, but to alert others that are armed to react.

Armed congregants inside the building is another matter. Here the better option is for trained guards or law enforcement to deal with a shooter, but some think that can be supplemented or even replaced by armed congregants.

Professional Guards

Professional Guards are well-trained, licensed professionals who usually have a military or police background or who are off-duty policemen and women.

Religious organizations hire both armed and unarmed guards.

Unarmed guards are (sometimes) trained to use various techniques to subdue an intruder. Some unarmed guards may carry chemical agents or even Tasers in certain jurisdictions. Most security guards carry handcuffs.

Many states license guards for hire[34], and some require training, but often training requirements are limited. In New York, for example, it includes 8 hours of introductory training and 16 hours of supervised training on the job. Formal training often is done through vocational institutes and usually there are required refresher training courses to maintain certification.

There have been complaints[35] that armed guards, particularly those hired from security companies, are not always well trained and sometimes there is no oversight of them by their employers.

There is a considerable deterrence benefit for guards, whether armed or not, to be dressed in uniforms and equipped with standard police paraphernalia and radio communications.

It is important for security guards to have proper protection, especially protective vests that protect against gunshots and attacks with knives or other weapons (such as box cutters that were used by the September 11, 2001 terrorists).

- **TAKE NOTE:** When hiring guards, **wearing protective vests should be required** in the contract for service. Consideration should be given on whether a congregation should just require or also purchase and require the use of protective vests.
- **TAKE NOTE:** Failure to require a protective vest could, in the case of an injury or death, lead to possible legal action against the congregation.

There are many reputable security companies who offer guards for hire. Some are local and others national. It is important to check the performance of any security company and sometimes local police can be helpful in evaluating the hiring of security guards.

It is important to have enough guards to provide coverage of a property and for one to back up the other in case of a crisis. At minimum two guards are needed: one at the front or main entrance and the other patrolling the perimeter.

Guards should work with volunteers to extend their surveillance capability and have early warning of any potential threat.

IMPORTANT: Guards also need access to various cameras and sensors both on the perimeter and inside the building(s). Today with cameras connected wirelessly to Wi-Fi networks, handheld devices such as tablets and mobile phones can give guards a much better real-time picture of the facility—what the military like to call "situational awareness." Caution, however should be used in relying on cameras and sensors for operational intelligence. Watching a monitor or screen can detract from one's security awareness.

Security Guards can make a big difference.

On June 17th, 2019 a terrorist armed with three knives attempted to enter two synagogues[36] in the Belgian city of Antwerp during the two-day Jewish holiday of Shavuot (Pentecost), but was stopped by alert security guards both times. The terrorist, a man reportedly of Iraqi descent, pretended to be Jewish, wearing a skull cap.

Parking Lots and Access Roads

In suburban and rural areas, religious sites often have their own parking lot, and sometimes access roads leading to them. Even in some cities, there may be some parking facilities for congregants. Intruders, it should be kept in mind do not typically arrive at a targeted site by public transportation or by walking. Frequently they bring their (owned, rented, stolen) vehicles. If they have free access to parking lots without supervision, this gives them an easy way to blend in with others walking into a church, mosque, temple or synagogue; and it gives them a rapid exit to get away after an active shooting or other such event.

There are additional reasons to patrol parking areas.

One is to protect congregants from assaults in parking lots. There are many cases of active shooters, especially where there is some sort of grievance or domestic issue, which may start in a parking lot and spread into the temple itself. This is what happened at the Pilgrim Valley Church, at 4800 S. Riverside Drive in Fort Worth, Texas when a violent argument broke out in the church's parking lot and soon spread to the church itself. Another shooting happened at Christ the Redeemer Catholic Church in Cypress, a Houston suburb, which took place in the parking lot. In Anderson, Indiana a teenager was arrested for shooting another teen in the parking lot of the South Meridian Church of God, a shooting caused by a dispute over illegal drugs.

Likewise, there is the risk of robberies and sexual assaults in parking lots, especially when there isn't any illumination on evenings. Many religious institutions hold meetings and events at night time. One report says[37] in nine out of 10 cases women are the victims of assaults, but it seems they are especially vulnerable in parking lots.

In Union, South Carolina a 20-year-old woman was raped in a parking lot behind the Union Presbyterian church.

In Oklahoma City, a deaf woman pedestrian[38] was kidnapped by a rapist, but the rape occurred in a dark, church parking lot.

Ronald L. Lineberger, 46, was charged with two counts of rape, sexual assault, making terroristic threats and simple assault of a 29-year-old woman that took place in a church parking lot in Mercer County, Pennsylvania, not far from Youngstown, Ohio.

Emanuel Kidega Samson was charged with murder and multiple counts of attempted murder[39] in the attack that killed one and left at least seven other people injured at the Burnette Chapel Church of Christ in Antioch, a town just south of Nashville, Tennessee. A Nashville Police Department spokesman said the shooter entered the church wearing a neoprene ski mask. One woman was shot in the parking lot before the shooter entered the church and opened fire on about 42 people still inside.

Many cases of assault are not reported or only show up in local newspapers. Often the perpetrators get away and are never apprehended.

Parking lots, especially in after-hour settings, can shield burglars and vandals where they can destroy property, set fires, put graffiti on walls, or place bombs.

Patrolling parking lots and installing motion detectors, cameras and other sensors in parking lots are useful ways to reduce the opportunity for a rapist, burglar, vandal or killer to use adjacent parking lots as a jumping off point for crime. Good lighting is important and loud alarms can scare off an attacker.

In parking lots, occasional armed guard or police patrols plus the use of volunteers are helpful steps.

Emergency call boxes in parking lots also can be effective.

Where parking is physically attached to the main building or to school buildings, a gated parking lot with key card entrance is a useful and effective precaution.

Gated communities in the US and elsewhere are increasingly common, and there is no reason why churches, mosques, temples and synagogues should not have similar protection.

IMPORTANT: Don't neglect parking lot security!

Bomb Threats and Parking

The threat of a bomb can never be lightly dismissed. In today's world, where bombings of churches, synagogues, mosques and temples around the world occur more and more often, the danger of bombing has to be understood as the modern reality.

In Mahabothi Temple in Bodh, Gaya, India ten bombs exploded, probably set by an Islamic terror group. One of the bombs was placed behind the door of a children's classroom. Three other bombs that did not explode were also discovered.

In the Philippines, at Our Lady of Mount Carmel Cathedral in Jolo, on January 27, 2019 bombs killed 23 people and wounded nearly 100 others. The bombs were set by Abu Sayyaf[40] militants.

In Bloomington, Minnesota a pipe bomb was tossed into the Dar Al Farooq Islamic Center by an anti-government group that calls itself the White Rabbit Militia.

Damon Joseph, 21, said that he wanted to kill a rabbi and bomb a synagogue. Joseph spent months talking about and planning a mass shooting of a Toledo-area synagogue and said he wanted to kill as many people as possible, including a rabbi.

Damon Joseph, 21, said that he wanted to kill a rabbi. (U.S. Department of Justice photo)

Bombs can be placed in automobiles, trucks, carried on bicycles or baby strollers, or hidden in backpacks and packages. Backpacks are often favoured by radical Islamic terrorists. When an unknown package is spotted, it is important to keep people as far away as possible from the object and it is imperative to summon police using 911, warning of a possible bomb, so the bomb squad can also come to the scene.

Spotting a Suspicious Package

The New York Police Department[41] (NYPD) gives the following advice for packages sent in the mail:

Look for a lack of a return address, restrictive markings like "personal," "overnight delivery," or "do not x-ray." Other indicators include poor typing or misspelled names and addresses, or the wrong or misspelled title and name on the package.

Other possible indicators include a rigid or bulky envelope, excessive postage, envelopes sealed with excessive amounts of tape, protruding wires, and oily stains on the wrapping, a strange odor or lopsided packaging.

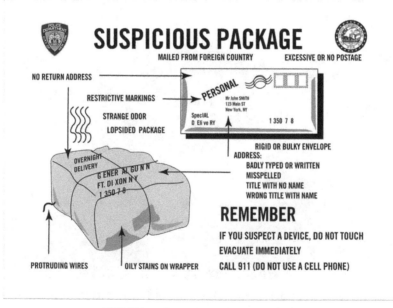

NYPD Slide on Recognizing a Suspicious Package

For bombs that are placed around the exterior of a building or hidden in a vehicle, it is not always easy to recognize them. The first rule is that any package that is where it shouldn't be (such as a box, a suitcase, backpack, brief case or an unidentified vehicle) contact police immediately and stay clear of the package or vehicle.

IMPORTANT: Leaders will need to make a decision whether or not to evacuate a building or parts of a building that are near the source of the threat.

Prudence dictates evacuation is the most responsible course of action, even if doing so will disrupt religious services or school instruction. The old adage, "Better Safe than Sorry" applies here.

Registering Vehicles

Keep in mind that a bomb can be hidden in a "strange" car or truck.

If there is a vehicle you do not know that is in your parking lot or a parking area adjacent to your buildings, inform the police. One way to confirm whether the vehicle is "strange" or not, is to page the congregation and ask whether a vehicle with thus and such license plate belongs to any of them.

It is a useful idea, even in parking lots that are nominally open to have congregants register their vehicles and carry either a parking sticker or at least register their number (license) plate with the congregation and building security.

Parking signs should make clear that only registered vehicles are permitted and others will be towed to an impoundment lot.

The Danger of Assault by Vehicle

One of the greatest dangers to a holy place is an explosive-laden vehicle that is driven into the building from a street or roadway, even from a parking lot.

The truck attack on the Christmas Market in Berlin on December 19, 2016 was truly horrifying, but not unexpected. The German authorities had clear warnings of attacks on Christmas markets for weeks. But could they have done anything to prevent such an attack? The fact is they did next to nothing and Germans and foreign tourists paid the deadly price. (It was only after the incident that the city installed cement road barriers—called Jersey barriers—that could prevent a car or truck from driving into the Christmas market area.)

In Nice, France a truck attack on July 16, 2016 on Bastille Day could have been prevented had the police protection of road barriers been kept in place[42] until people attending a celebratory parade in that city had time to go home. But the police barriers were removed prematurely exposing Nice's citizens and visitors to an attack by a large truck that proved very hard for the police to stop.

In the aftermath, some police were complaining that the barriers were taken down too early or that there was an insufficient presence of police at the scene. It is known, for example, that the refrigerated, 19-ton van used in the attack, which was leased, was not permitted on the roadway. Even so, the driver made four practice runs up and down the promenade road before the barriers were put in place without anyone taking notice.

In Germany, the authorities—despite the warnings—did very little to protect Christmas markets like the one at Breitscheidplatz Square, outside the Kaiser Wilhelm Memorial Church in the German capital's main shopping area. There the hijacked, Polish-owned van ran down pedestrians and market stalls, hitting them at a speed of 40 mph.

The area could have been protected by heavy, cement Jersey barriers put there on a temporary basis. There was adequate room to place such barriers. A ten-foot Jersey barrier section weighs almost 5,000 pounds. Because they feature curved sides, Jersey barriers are used on roadways to protect against vehicles "jumping" lanes, including trucks. While not a perfect solution, temporary Jersey barriers would have likely saved lives. Another alternative would be permanent cable barriers along the periphery of the Christmas Markets. Had there been a desire to install them, there was time between the warnings received of a threat to Christmas Markets and the December 19th attack.

The US warned Germany of the high risk of attacks on Christmas Markets on November 22nd[43]. "The US State Department said it had "credible information" that Islamic State of Iraq and the Levant[44] (ISIL or ISIS) and al-Qaeda were planning attacks and focusing on the "upcoming holiday season." American tourists were explicitly warned to avoid Christmas markets. It is astonishing that there was only minimal security in place to protect these locations.

The German newspaper Die Welt (as reported in the London Daily Mail[45]) said: "ISIS had, in recent weeks, had made renewed calls for disciples to carry out atrocities in Europe and German intelligence warned Berlin authorities recently that the city's bustling markets – tourist magnets for foreigners— were vulnerable to attack."

The alleged suspect was a Tunisian asylum seeker named Anis Amri[46]. He was closely tied to ISIS through Tunisian allied terror organizations. The German police are said to have been tracking him, but "lost" him.

According to the London Daily Mail[47], the "Tunisian asylum seeker suspected of carrying out Berlin massacre was arrested THREE times [in 2016 before the Christmas market attack]amid fears he was planning a terror plot— but police [in Germany] let him go and [offered] €100,000 euros ($111,229) to anyone who [located] him." It also turns out Amri got into Europe through Italy along with others who claimed they were Syrian refugees. In Italy, he set fire to a school and was jailed for four years. How he wound up in Germany after serving his jail term in Italy is not known, but he went there after leaving jail. No one stopped him: there are no borders inside Europe. It is likely he was connected to terrorist cells in Germany.

When it comes to security to try and prevent attacks, the more security forces are visible and present, the less likely an attack will be carried out. The objective of ISIS-led attacks, like other terrorist-led operations, is to inflict maximum casualties and create a horror that will destabilize governments and undermine the confidence citizens have in law enforcement. Obviously, the lack of any visible deterrent characterized the Christmas market attack in Berlin and this made it a prime target for terror organizations.

It is no small thing to stop a speeding truck. The truck used in the Berlin attack was a 25-ton vehicle, and it was packed with a load of steel girders that were supposed to be delivered to customers in Berlin. All reports to date show that the truck was hijacked. The trucking company owner says he lost contact with the driver (his cousin) and could not reach him. The truck had stopped and started a number of times and was not being driven correctly[48]. Unfortunately, so far as is known, the errant truck was not reported by the owner to authorities so police in Berlin had no information that a truck had possibly been hijacked or that a truck had gone missing that was heading to Berlin (based on a GPS unit in the truck itself). Had authorities been alerted, they could have located the truck and stopped it well short of the terrorist's target.

One useful step that law enforcement in Europe should have implemented would be an alert system on the location of vehicles. Trucking inside the European Union (as in the United States) is closely regulated so the potential exists to track these vehicles and warn if routes are abridged or other unusual information reaches trucking company managers. The fact the truck in the Berlin attack was modern, equipped with GPS[49] and monitoring equipment, indicates that the trucking company could have reported the situation to law enforcement when the truck apparently went missing. But to bring this into focus, law enforcement would need to have put out a bulletin or warning to trucking companies explaining the risks and asking them for any unusual information.

Above all it seems that passing on warnings did not result in any action by police or Berlin officials.

How to protect sanctuaries and religious schools from vehicular assault

---

IMPORTANT: Make sure barriers can protect against trucks as well as cars.

In some cases, placing large "decorative" boulders strategically is enough to stop a speeding vehicle.

In other places, where boulders are inappropriate or where the religious institution is located in an urban setting, the use of bollards is recommended.

A bollard is a short vertical post, generally made of steel and anchored firmly into the ground. Well-designed bollards can protect against vehicles crashing into them.

In the United States, the Defense Department and State Department set anti-terrorism standards for protection against terrorist attacks. These standards are widely used in the broader community to assess security products. Elsewhere the ASTM (formerly the American Society for Testing and Materials) International Standard is used.

Both domestic US and international standards rate bollards by the speed and weight of an approaching vehicle and by the amount of penetration protection afforded by the bollard.

Bollards can either be fixed in the ground or, where desired, bollards can be hydraulically lifted into place and raised and lowered as needed. For example, bollards can protect an area but be lowered to allow access to a cleared delivery truck.

There is extensive information online[50] as to how bollards are rated.

On May 20, 2017 Richard Rojas[51], a 26-year Bronx resident, intentionally drove onto the sidewalk in Times Square, New York in an attempt to "kill them all," he told police, according to a criminal complaint. He was charged with murder and 20 counts of attempted murder. His vehicle ran into sidewalk bollards which wrecked his vehicle and prevented him from carrying out the attack. He was subdued by two courageous citizens.

Image showing bollards where Rojas' car was impaled.
(By Epicgenius - Own work, Creative Commons, Public Domain)

Bollards are by no means the only way to prevent a vehicle from crashing into a building.

Cement and water-filled dense plastic barriers can also stop vehicles, are relatively inexpensive and usually are heavy enough to not require anchoring.

Cable barriers—thick steel cables anchored into the ground (sometimes hidden in sidewalk flower boxes made of bricks) can also stop virtually any vehicle if the cables are properly anchored.

A roadway type cable security barrier. Note the steel posts are anchored in cement and the cable at each end is also anchored. (Photo by Mazzella Companies)

Windows and Glass

A drive-by shooter can spray an entranceway firing through plate glass windows and doorways.

A pipe bomb or other explosive device can shatter the windows of a meeting room or even the main sanctuary, spraying glass fragments that can kill and maim.

Different strategies are needed to deal with shooting through plate glass and dealing with flying glass from bombings.

Drive-by shootings are usually focused on a building entrance, and the most vulnerable are those with plate glass windows or doors.

Consider the case of Philip Manshaus, 22 of Oslo, Norway who was subdued after crashing into the al-Noor mosque's glass door in an affluent suburb of Oslo, Norway on August 10, 2019. Manshaus is a self-proclaimed Nazi. Later his adopted sister, Johanne Zhangjin Ihle-Hansen was found dead in her car, shot in the head. She was of Asian descent. Had the congregants failed to subdue him immediately, he would have killed many. He was armed with two shotguns and a third gun was recovered later. Had the door been made of sturdier material, Manshaus would not have been able to enter the mosque.

Bulletproof glass is often made from acrylic material, and cost-effective glass replacements can be purchased for doors and entrance windows that will be effective against 9 mm and super 38 semi-automatic handguns with a muzzle energy of 380 to 460 foot-pounds. This material probably won't help against a high-powered rifle, but drive-by shooters typically use easy-to-aim weapons or semi-automatics that shoot small rounds.

Below is a photo of the murder of Anthony Soares in Toronto, who was shot by handguns through a glass doorway.

Two Gunmen Shooting through Glass Doors Killing Anthony Soares (An image from a Toronto police released video, the victim's image is obscured by the Police before releasing image)

Because it is typical to have a greeter or guard inside the front door, if there is a glass door this individual is immediately at risk even before an active shooter penetrates the building.

It is also fairly likely that congregants will be gathered in the hallways leading to the sanctuary, which means many could be at risk from an active shooter.

IMPORTANT: Glass entrances and large windows at the entrance or elsewhere at ground level should be replaced with bullet proof glass.

Flying Glass

The Federal Emergency Management Agency (FEMA) says that lacerations due to high-velocity, flying glass have been responsible for a significant portion of the injuries received in explosion incidents.

Flying glass, propelled by an explosion, fragments, lacerates and penetrates the body of victims.

Laceration and penetration wounds require immediate treatment to prevent victims going into shock or bleeding out.

Flying glass along with other debris and collapsing structures is a major challenge for First Responders.

There are at least three ways to minimize the danger of flying glass.

Perhaps the most popular today are special films that can be put over window glass that resist shattering in case there is an explosion.

Such films must be anchored to the window frame or they will not work correctly. What they do is act as a sort of fragment catching net, and will expand outward in a blast, but will stay anchored for long enough to prevent glass shards from being propelled inward.

Security films have another benefit: if someone tries to break through glass that has the film installed, it can make it far harder for an intruder to do so. The company 3-M says their film will take about 45 seconds before it can be penetrated. LLumar security films also provide similar protection. Providing there are breakage sensors connected to an alarm system, this could help in warning off an intruder where his or her intent was to smash and grab and run.

LLumar protective window film showing an attempt to break glass with film installed (LLumar photo)

It makes sense to install films of this type on exterior classroom windows, especially at ground level, and on sanctuary glass such as large, plate glass windows or stained glass.

The security film does not take away from the opacity of the glass while providing a much-enhanced level of security.

The film can be used on bulletproof doors enhancing protection.

Another approach is to replace glass with specially laminated glass, which is similar to automobile windshield glass, a sort of sandwich of glass and a plastic or Mylar material. Just as in an automobile, safety glass prevents shattering (instead the glass crumbles), laminated glass will do the same in a building. The main drawback is that laminated glass is quite expensive and requires that existing window glass be completely removed and replaced. Laminated glass is not bulletproof.

Finally, there are blast curtains which, when shut work a lot like protective window film in that they act as a shard catching net.

Blast curtains usually are employed in high security government and military structures and are not so common in civil applications.

Fencing and Gates

Security fencing and strong locked gates are important in protecting sensitive areas around a structure, particularly schools and playgrounds, as well as day care centers.

In older churches and some synagogues, particularly those in towns and cities, often are traditionally protected by iron fences and gates to adjacent courtyards. Sometimes there is a gate at the front entrance, but during church or synagogue activity the gates are often left open.

Today, many modern house of worship buildings, particularly in suburban and rural areas, lack gates or fences.

Fences and locking gates can be useful, nonetheless. For example, protected play areas for children and access to sensitive areas can benefit from strong fences and gates, although in no case is a gate or fence by itself enough to stop an active threat.

Playgrounds

Many religious organizations have play areas for children that are outside. The danger, of course, is that children could be exposed to any number of threats, including shooting, vehicular assaults, bombings and kidnapping. Strong and resilient fencing can help protect kids from vehicular assaults and kidnapping.

WARNING: Playgrounds should always have adult supervision and adults should be capable of rapidly evacuating a playground area in case of any perceived threat. This includes removing children immediately if persons outside the fence attempt to engage children in conversation.

Similarly, fencing can help protect areas around a building that are sensitive, such as the main sanctuary or school classrooms.

Gates can also help regulate traffic, especially the entry of delivery vehicles by forcing them to wait at a checkpoint where the vehicle can be validated by staff.

Unless gates are exceptionally strong, they may not be able to stop a car or truck that is used to ram a building or congregants, including children. Stronger physical barriers, including professionally installed bollards or heavy rocks or other suitable barrier is a more effective protection.

Life Cycle Events

Many life cycle events take place at a house of worship, and even funerals may need some kind of protection. An assault at a funeral is not just a phenomena that happens in the Middle East, where terrorists may disrupt a funeral service or a burial. It happens also in the United States.

On April 20, 2019 two people were injured after a shooting outside a funeral at the Jackson Chapel United Methodist Church in Frederick,

Maryland. The shooting took place in the church's parking lot while the funeral service proceeded.

In 2018, a man was fatally shot at the funeral for his younger brother in Baltimore. This shooting actually occurred at the cemetery.

In June, 2018 five people were wounded at a funeral home-cemetery on the Hayward-Union City border in the San Francisco Bay area.

In Chicago six people were shot as they exited the Bethlehem Star Church where they attended the funeral of Vantrease Criss, a rapper also known as "Dooskie the Man."

ABC-7 in Chicago reported that Pastor Roosevelt Watkins was at the back of the church when the shots began. He described the scene unfolding outside.

"It was pandemonium. People ducking under cars, running for their lives, for safety, running back inside of the church, trying to get out of harm's way," Watkins said.

"It sounded more or less like at least 40-50 gunshots from our backyard. And we came right away, there was gun shelling back here, there was blood on the floor. Right away the ambulance and the police came, immediately," said Ruth Rivera, who lives nearby.

Sherri Savage owns Chesterfield Tom Thumb Day Care Center, which is located across the street from where the shooting happened. The facility had about 25 children inside and was placed on lockdown.

Shootings at churches also happen during happier events. KSAT-TV in San Antonio[52] reported that on March 18, 2019 gunfire erupted outside the Holy Spirit Catholic Church during a wedding reception. According to police, two men left the scene in a white Ford pickup truck and one man was left wounded. The man, later identified as Marcos Villegas-Martinez, died at a local hospital. Security at the church asked the two men to leave who were having an argument with a third man. They did so, but they shot Villegas-Martinez from their vehicle as he left the church.

Umberto Ferreira dos Santos, known by his nickname Betinho, opened fire at guests at a wedding ceremony inside the Our Lady of Conception church in Limoeiro de Anadia, in Brazil. He actually walked down the aisle behind the bride and groom, pulled out a handgun and started shooting.

There were three victims: Cicero Barbosa da Silva, 62, his son Edmilson Bezerra da Silva, 37, and his wife (not named). They were guests at the wedding.

According to the UK Daily Mail, witnesses said Dos Santos (the shooter) parked his car in front of the church and walked to the front of the church. He accused Edmilson of being responsible for the death of his son before shooting each of the three victims once.

Conclusion

- Perimeter security (the space outside a building or buildings) is the first line of defense against a threat to a congregation.
- Most physical attacks (other than some bombings) generally assault the easiest access point, and this is usually the main entrance.
- While a guard is a deterrent, if the guard is unarmed or is elderly or is just a volunteer from the congregation, the chances to actually stop a determined intruder is not very good.
- Volunteers usually are unarmed, but may wear safety vests and certainly must carry radios that can communicate with the armed guards present at a location and local police (where permitted).
- Perimeter security should begin at the building operating entrance (which may not be the front doors). Unless guards can be put in place at alternative entry points (such as a side door), congregants and others should only be able to enter through the operating entrance or through special needs entrances that also are monitored.
- There is risk at special needs entrances that a shooter could try and enter immediately behind a special needs individual.
- Attention should be paid to the curb areas and walkways around an entrance, since congregants can be vulnerable entering or leaving

a house of worship. Dangers include drive by shooting, vehicular ramming and physical assault.

- Close communications between volunteers and security guards is a very important enhancement for the chance to head off an incident. This includes wireless panic buttons in the hands of volunteers capable of summoning armed guards.

- Where armed volunteers are permitted, and where they are properly trained and protected (for example by security vests), they can provide significant protection on the perimeter, although their service is not without significant risks.

- Professional Guards are well-trained, licensed professionals who usually have a military or police background or who are off-duty policemen and women.

- There are many cases of active shooters, especially where there is some sort of grievance or domestic issue, which may start in a parking lot and spread into the temple itself.

- Dark parking lots, especially in after-hour settings, can shield burglars and vandals from destroying property, setting fires, painting graffiti on walls, or placing bombs. Dark parking lots are sometimes the scene of other crimes including rape and murder.

- When an unknown package is spotted, it is important to keep people as far away as possible from the object or evacuate them and it is imperative to summon police using 911, warning of a possible bomb so the bomb squad can also come to the scene.

- It is a useful idea, even in parking lots that are nominally open to have congregants register their vehicles and carry either a parking sticker or at least register their number (license) plate with the congregation and security. In addition, parking signs should make clear that only registered vehicles are permitted and others will be towed to an impoundment lot.

- One of the greatest dangers to a holy place is an explosive-laden vehicle that is driven into the building from a street or roadway, even from a parking lot.

- Most important of all is to make sure there are barriers that even a large truck can't penetrate which can be accomplished by large rocks, bollards and other barriers. Vehicles have been used to run down citizens in the United States and elsewhere.
- Because it is typical to have a greeter or guard inside the front door, if there is a glass door this individual is immediately at risk even before an active shooter penetrates the building. Consideration should be given to bulletproof glass at entrances that have glass doors or windows.
- The Federal Emergency Management Agency (FEMA) says that lacerations due to high-velocity flying glass have been responsible for a significant portion of the injuries received in explosion incidents.
- Special films that can be put over window glass that resist shattering in case there is an explosion can save many lives. Probably half the injuries in an explosion come from flying debris, especially glass shards.
- Security fencing and strong, locked gates are important in protecting sensitive areas around a structure, particularly schools and playgrounds, as well as day care centers.
- Playgrounds should always have adult supervision and adults should be capable of rapidly evacuating a playground area in case of any perceived threat. This includes removing children immediately if persons outside the fence attempt to engage children in conversation.
- Many life event festivities take place at houses of worship, and even funerals may need some kind of extra security protection

CHAPTER 5

Interior Security

Before you Begin

In assessing interior vulnerabilities you should start with a good building diagram of the interior, including all levels of the structure.

The diagram will have to take into account different building levels, stairways, and internal and external doorways. All exits need to be clearly marked.

You need to know where the main electrical box is located, where fire extinguishers are positioned, and if there is natural gas in the building, where the main shutoff valve is.

The diagram should show where guards are currently stationed inside the building (as in an entrance hallway).

Interior CCTV cameras (and their coverage areas) need to be checked.

Fire alarm locations need to be identified and the alarm circuits should be checked by the local fire marshal.

Door locks and strength and condition of internal doorways must be noted (to facilitate lock down procedures).

If there are interior locks on doorways they need to be identified (and the type specified). If doors can be locked automatically that should be referenced.

Fire extinguishers need to be identified, their location(s) marked, and extinguishers checked to make sure they are current. Fire extinguishers need to be replaced or recharged because over time they will lose their charge and not work properly.

Access to medical supplies and equipment (such as defibrillators) should be checked both for availability and operations and a determination made if supplies are adequate. Defibrillators should be in a hallway visible to all congregants and staff.

Supplemental oxygen supplies, stretchers and other gear should be assessed (if available). It is likely there are congregants who have a medical or nursing background. Take advantage of their expertise to assess what supplies are available and what should be added.

Medical supplies should be on hand to deal with a large-scale emergency such as a fire, explosion, bombing or shooting and for "routine" incidents such as heart attacks, injuries caused by accidents or falls, etc.

Blankets are needed which can help to snuff out fires and keep people warm in cold weather or experiencing shock.

Access points to use public address systems should be noted (if a public address system is installed).

Location(s) of sirens and alarms must be marked on the diagram.

Orthodox Jewish Considerations

For many Orthodox Jewish congregations (and some Jewish conservative congregations) the Sabbath and many Jewish holidays are considered especially holy and Jews in those congregations are not supposed to use automobiles or do any work (even flipping a light switch is considered work).

This has created a conundrum for some congregations in figuring out how to do security which requires technology (such as radios, activating alarms, using a public address system) and interventionary action.

Many congregations, accounting for the nature of modern-day threats have used a biblical principle known in Hebrew as Pikuach Nefesh, which means "to save a life" is a justification to allow staff and volunteers from the congregation to do what is necessary for security. (See: Leviticus 18:5 where it is believed in a close reading and interpretation that people should live by the law and not die by it.)

Pikuach Nefesh can be interpreted to allow gun-carry and other actions (such as the use of force) to protect the lives of the congregation.

There are many different interpretations of Pikuach Nefesh. It is up to the affected congregations and their religious leadership to decide what is acceptable to them.

Similarly some Christian communities oppose violence so much so that they won't have armed guards.

This issue came up concerning the prestigious Sidwell Friends School which was attended by President Barak Obama's two daughters. Sidwell Friends is a Quaker school that preaches non-violence and pacifism. It has unarmed guards but no armed guards. A compromise of sorts was reached when President Obama's children attended the school. Secret Service personnel stationed at the school were armed. Similarly, a Jewish school in the Washington DC area where President Trump's daughter and son-in-laws children attended, had only unarmed guards. Again the Secret Service provided armed protection for the children.

While there are those who advocate reliance on unarmed guards, in both cases of the President's children and grandchildren, armed guards were put in place as a proper precaution.

Interior versus Perimeter Protection

Securing the inside of a building, especially a religious location is more difficult than making the outer perimeter safe.

That's because if an intruder is at all familiar with the internal layout of the structure, he will immediately head for the target area which, in most instances is the main sanctuary.

Typical church, synagogue, mosque and temple sanctuaries have very little protection and once an intruder gets past the guard or guards, he is free to complete his planned operation, which usually involves shooting and killing.

Some churches in particular are especially vulnerable because the sanctuary proper is open to the outside. Typically, there is a small open vestibule where devotional candles, incense or coat racks are located, but where the church service is still open and visible.

One consideration is to not use the front or main entrance, but to channel congregants through a side or rear door where guards can better control who enters and can block or lock down even the main sanctuary in an emergency.

The available options depend strongly on the physical layout of the building.

Even if a front entrance is used, there are ways to slow down access to the main sanctuary.

Metal Detectors

One good security procedure is to place a metal detector at the front entrance or alternative entrance and channel all visitors through it.

This will create a slowdown in entering the facility, a kind of *benevolent bottleneck*, affording security the chance to identify, intercept and isolate a threat. Without the benevolent bottleneck, the facility would be exposed to an active threat with little chance to deal with it.

A metal detector and bag inspection should also be part of the operational strategy if a side or rear entrance is used.

Anything that can aid in identifying a potential threat is a positive way of isolating the threat and gives security an opportunity to protect against an intruder.

Some synagogues and a few churches already inspect bags, backpacks or don't allow them at all, and use metal detectors of some type.

The type of sensor most people are familiar with are those they see at airports or in government buildings. They are often tied to X-ray machines to inspect bags, and sometimes to explosive detectors (sniffers).

Today, metal detectors can be sized for nearly any entrance and some can be moved out of the way when not needed. There are attractive, slim-line designs available. Magnetic sensors can operate on standard power outlets or by battery.

Metal detectors are also available in hand-held wands which are battery powered. These however are not as effective as in place detectors and take time and experience to use correctly.

The Department of Homeland Security has published a Patron Screening Best Practices Guide[53] that has useful advice on the "do's" and "don'ts" for effective screening of patrons. Of course, church congregants are not exactly patrons in the commercial sense of the word, but the guidance still is valuable and worth consulting.

Using a metal detector won't catch every threat. If a wand type sensor is used, the security officer may not do a thorough check or the wand may be triggered off by non-threatening items such as cellular phones and car keys. And package inspection, whether manually done or with a machine may not catch every item.

While metal detectors have some weaknesses and bag inspections are not always thorough enough, along with identifying a weapon, knife or explosive, the metal detector also functions as another benevolent bottleneck.

Slowing down an intruder can force the potential threat to –in effect— show his hand. By getting an early indication of an active shooter or similar threat, the chance to quickly isolate the threat and allows security to take steps to protect against the threat.

For example, according to the New York Post[54], Historic Trinity Church and St. Paul's Chapel have installed metal detectors at their entrances, citing terrorism fears. A sign posted in time for Lent instructs visitors to empty their pockets and warns: "Please note that weapons are not permitted inside the church."

The Post reported that "Four guards manned the detectors at the entrance to Trinity and two more greeted visitors inside the church last week in the days leading to Palm Sunday. An additional two guards and another metal detector were stationed at a second entrance."

Hand held detectors are less effective than walk through metal detectors, but they have the advantage that they can be used anywhere easily, even outdoors. Like metal detectors, visible hand held detectors are a deterrent.

Random Bag Inspections and Body Searches

Random bag search and body searches using magnetometers can be a strategy where there are limited personnel or where most of the congregants are known to volunteers and security guards.

There are two downsides to this approach: the first is that the deterrent effect of a consistent check on all visitors (whether regulars or not) is lost because an intruder may not see the chance of being checked as a significant impediment.

The second problem is that random checks lose the benevolent bottleneck that helps guards stop a threat.

Another shortcoming is that a known congregant can sometimes be the shooter! This has happened enough times, because of some grievance either with another congregant, a staff member, minister, Imam, or rabbi or a grievance with the church itself.

Finally, there is the issue of a mentally ill or deranged member of the congregation who could bring a weapon with him or her to a church, mosque, temple or synagogue. Because random searches may often skip "known" members of a congregation and focus on unknown visitors, such a person would slip through.

According to the Allentown Morning Call[55] newspaper, in Springfield Township, Pennsylvania a woman who attended the Trinity Evangelical Lutheran Church became infatuated with the Church's pastor, even though he rebuffed her advances. When the woman, Mary Jane Fonder, suspected that a fellow congregant and choir singer might have been having her own affair with the pastor, "she shot the woman twice in the head inside an office at the Springfield church." The victim, who did not survive was Rhonda Smith, 42, of Hellertown, Pennsylvania.

There are enough examples of disputes and mental problems that affect religious institutions to exercise care in granting free or easy access to any member of the congregation.

Wherever possible, consistent use of metal detectors and bag searches is overall the best policy to follow.

WARNING: If concealed carry weapons are allowed in a holy place, some means of preregistration and verification is advisable.

Lockdown or Evacuation?

Most public schools in the United States use lockdown when there is a threat in or near the school building. This is known as a "Code Red" alert procedure. Code Red is the most severe and stringent form of alert, and the school is totally locked down and children confined to locked classrooms.

In cases where students must stay in their classrooms, but where normal classroom work continues is known as a "Code Yellow."

A "Code Blue" is for a medical emergency where paramedics or other health personnel are urgently needed.

School lockdowns work because classrooms are typically spaces that are protected by a door.

Doors are designed so they can be secured from inside the classroom, usually by a deadbolt lock that can be manually engaged. Some schools may have electronic door locks that are activated centrally in a Code Red situation.

The classroom doors themselves have to be strong enough so they can't be pushed or kicked in.

Doors with standard glass are not adequate to secure a classroom.

Many classroom doors in modern schools have a small, generally vertical glass panel, which, for security, should be replaced with anchored Plexiglas. Some schools are going to bulletproof glass panels or alternatively to complete hardened security doors for classrooms, common areas and school libraries and offices.

Some schools feature so-called Open Classrooms, where students work in an open environment. Open Classrooms have some educational advantages, it is said, but from a security perspective they make security more difficult.

Many churches, synagogues and other religious sites have classrooms and meeting rooms that can be locked down provided the right types of locks are installed and the doors are sturdy. (Some schools are installing bullet-resistant doors.)

The primary issue is an alert mechanism, which can be a siren or warning bell, or a public address system. Schools had public address systems long before most of them practiced lock downs. These were typically used for announcements and for the start and conclusion of the school day.

Schools today may also send phone texts to parents when there is a lockdown. Parents are advised not to come to the school but to stand by for more information. Schools today recognize that many students have mobile phones and will be calling or texting family and friends.

Some religious schools may do the same as a public school. But smaller schools for young children or specialized instruction may lack a lockdown system. Yet, putting a lockdown system in place is inexpensive and usually does not require much engineering.

The same lockdown capability can be extended to meeting rooms, general purpose rooms and libraries inside houses of worship, or extended to living quarters and other components of a church campus.

Social Halls

Social halls are used for celebrations, for educational events, for town meetings, for lunches and dinners, dances, bingo, wedding receptions, Bar and Bat Mitzvahs, and many other purposes. Sometimes social halls support alternative religious services, or as a backup location for churches, synagogues and mosques that are undergoing renovations.

Social halls are large spaces adjacent to the main sanctuary, sometimes basement rooms and in other cases are in a separate building.

Most of the time social halls are not protected or guarded, though they should be.

Social halls may have their own entrance door or doors and exit doors typically at the rear of a social hall usually leading outside.

IMPORTANT: In an emergency, social halls can and should be locked down. This is the best strategy compared to trying to evacuate a social hall. The clear exception to this is fire or explosion where evacuation is the preferred alternative.

Evacuations always risk a certain amount of panic and are hard to control. Moreover, an **evacuation from a social hall has to be directed away from any threat**. Knowing exactly where the threat is in an evolving situation is a problem.

Social halls that operate at night or at times when the church itself is not conducting religious services should nonetheless have the same level of protection as a religious service, meaning that guards and volunteers are needed, bag checks and metal detectors should be in use, and where possible incoming guests should be checked against lists provided by the family or families of those celebrating an event, or by leaders for non-life cycle events.

Some social halls are used for bingo games, social organization meetings, boy scouts and girl scouts, veteran groups and other persons not necessarily associated with the congregation itself. In some cases the social halls are a revenue source.

Because the danger always exists of an incident, welcoming churches can ask participating outside groups to help pay for security services.

If a social hall cannot be protected by a lockdown procedure, the only alternative is evacuation.

It is important to assess the most practical way to evacuate a social hall, keeping in mind that evacuation may be needed in cases of fire or explosion or loss of power (lighting blackout). Emergency battery powered lighting and clearly identified exits are essential.

Evacuation Protocols

While evacuation may sound easy, it is not. The challenge is keep control of any evacuation process in order to prevent panic responses and minimize as much as possible any further danger to those being evacuated.

There are some challenges including dealing with disabled people, very old people, and keeping control of children.

It is a practical idea to have a megaphone available and assign a staff person or persons to manage the evacuation process.

Above all, a safe evacuation is only possible where trained personnel or trained volunteers are available to manage and direct the evacuation activity.

These same rules apply to sanctuary evacuations and evacuation from chapels and other places that cannot be easily secured by a lockdown.

Trained personnel and volunteers need to have radio communications and, preferably a bullhorn to manage the social hall population. Personnel need to be stationed in at least three places: at the exit point(s), at the rear of the exit(s), and outside, if possible, to guide the guests as they leave.

There is bound to be some difficulty, especially if family members or children are elsewhere in the facility. Volunteers and staff need to make it clear that until the situation is stabilized and an all clear is given, family members, including children cannot attempt to try and find missing family or friends.

In preparing an evacuation strategy, some alternative locations for reassembling guests should be identified and tested to make sure the location is accessible. For example, if a parking lot is filled with cars, it will be hard to control people who will almost certainly want to get in their vehicles and drive away. Because police and first responder including fire truck vehicles will be in the area or on their way, clogging roadways with exiting cars and other vehicles is not helpful and could obstruct life saving measures.

Therefore, alternative locations need to be reached by foot and be reasonably accessible for young and old alike. Consideration has to be given to wheelchairs and transporting the infirm who may need walkers or other kinds of assistance.

GOLDEN RULE: In an evacuation the golden rule is to leave no one behind.

Volunteers should ask for names of missing children, relatives or friends so that their location can be identified.

In a crisis situation first responders may move wounded or distressed people to medical facilities. They probably will not have time to process names or inform families.

Preplanning and evacuation maps are very important to ease the process of moving people to an alternative location.

If there are nearby open buildings (such as other churches, schools, government buildings, recreation centers) that are open and available, consider using them. In preparing a plan, visit with the directors or heads of those facilities to work out an emergency response program with them.

IMPORTANT: Make sure that police know where you move people, because if the police have sufficient manpower, they can provide protection for evacuees.

Consideration has to be given not only to the process, but also to environmental conditions. An evacuation in winter with snow and ice on the ground is an example of a problem that has to be faced. Emergency blankets, first aid material (especially bandages and tourniquets), CPR (cardiopulmonary resuscitation) training and triage training and the kinds of know-how and equipment needed, should be included in the planning process and form a component of the follow up once a plan is in place.

Special training is needed to handle individuals who may be in shock.

Congregational Training

Almost every school practices lockdown and conducts fire drills to help faculty, students and staff know what procedures to follow.

Churches, synagogues, temples and mosques need to do the same thing and also to post instructions on walls and doors and put information in book holders in pews where possible, just as airplanes put safety instructions in seat backs.

Practice drills have significant benefits.

- First, members of the house of worship will understand how they will be alerted, who will give them instructions and how they need to respond
- Second, volunteers and staff will gain an understanding of what works in their plan and what needs to be improved. For example, how long did it take to execute an evacuation (a simple stopwatch is an important tool here), the level of difficulty in controlling a crowd, deficits in supplies (blankets, medical supplies, stretchers, oxygen)
- Third, it is important to understand how vital information will reach volunteers and staff in an emergency situation. This is important because a blind evacuation could result in casualties if the result is to run head-first into an active shooter, or find out that the evacuation path is blocked by emergency vehicles, fire or other barrier
- Fourth, the drill should test communications with police and guards
- Fifth, the drill should test the alarm system and public address system
- Sixth, the congregation should practice evacuations at different times of day and night, both from the sanctuary and the social hall(s) or meeting rooms

INFORMATION FOR CLASSROOMS: it is important to instruct students in lockdown procedures, how to stay away from doorways and minimize exposure to gunshots from outside the classroom.

Students need to understand to wait for all clear alarms before leaving a lockdown classroom.

Most grade school students will already know what to do based on their experience in public and private schools. Younger pre-school students will need to be shown what to do.

CHAPTER 6

Religious Camps

There are different camp types—day camps, overnight camps and adult retreats. Sometimes, summer day camps are organized on church grounds; sometimes they use public spaces for camps. Overnight camps, with some exceptions, are typically located in natural areas, by lakes, woodlands, on the sea shore. Adult retreats often use campgrounds or remote church property, typically "away from" the hustle and bustle of daily affairs.

Many if not most YMCA's (Young Men's Christian Association, now known simply as "the Y") run summer day and overnight camps open to all religions and denominations. The Y is in over 10,000 neighbourhoods in the United States.

All camps share some common vulnerabilities: they often use the outdoors for camp activities such as sports, swimming, boating and other activities (concerts, dancing etc.), many are poorly protected by fences and guards, and often are in remote hard-to-reach places.

Camp security is slowly starting to improve, but there remains a lot of resistance in the camp world[56] to strong security.

The American Camping Association, covering all types of camps around the country suggests the following guidelines. According to ACA's research, there are 14,000 youth camps in the US, with 14 million participants attending camp each year. (The following is provided by the ACA)

- Assess the susceptibility of your campers to threats of kidnapping, international terrorism, domestic terrorism, and other dangers. With the help of a professional, consider the threat to your campers
- Take stock of your land and location
- Assess your need for fencing, lighting, and telephones or cell phones for emergency calls. If your camp is on a large amount of land, ask your security firm how they can patrol or protect the area, especially in areas that cannot be fenced in or that include hundreds of acres. Review the architectural and environmental layout of your buildings in proximity to one another to determine secure and insecure areas. In addition, consider your camp's nearness to cities, roads, or heavily forested areas
- If your camp is conducted in a public place, assess your neighbouring environment, including how you will protect your campers and staff from others who are near you, might cross your path, or intentionally invade your space
- Design a protocol for handling visitors. Your protocol for parents, whose visits are probably anticipated, will be different from that for sporadic visitors like delivery people
- Develop protocols for the acceptance and transfer of luggage, mail, and other parcels. Programs whose campers arrive by airplane have to deal with the handling of luggage in the airport. Contact the airport to create safe and low-hassle methods for transporting campers' luggage. Camps may be able to set up an arrangement with the local airport to allow staff to accompany campers to the boarding gate. Staff may then call campers' parents when campers board the plane and again when the plane takes off
- Assess the quality of security and control present in your facility, especially in the evenings. Some camps employ night-time officers or guard patrol. Others request that local law enforcement drive by at regular intervals

- Coordinate with local support systems. A camp might consider allowing local law enforcement to use their land for training when camp is not in session; this helps officers familiarize themselves with the grounds
- Help parents feel confident. Tell them about the safety and security measures you have in place, but don't undermine your security plan by divulging all the information

---

Jewish camps face some unique threats because they are targets for hate groups. Jews in Europe, the United States and Canada (and places as far afield as Australia, Turkey, and Russia) are faced with many anti-Israel, anti-Zionist and antisemitic threats that globally have been increasing.

In 2016, the Anti-Defamation League of the B'nai B'rith (Children of the Covenant) documented a dramatic 34% increase in antisemitic incidents, a number that has continued to rise during 2017. Jewish institutions and schools across the country are targets of vandalism and violent threats. Other minorities may face similar threats.

Likewise, according to the U.S. Department of Justice (DOJ), the incidence of violent crimes committed against and by children and youth continues to rise in America. This alarming data has youth-serving organizations on full alert and continually reviewing and increasing their security measures.

To date, there has not been an actual terrorist attack on a Jewish camp either in the United States or Canada, although many camps have beefed up security.

In the summer of 2012, several intruders drove through Camp Bonim, a religious boy's camp in rural Pennsylvania, according to local police who later arrested five suspects. In 2015, it was Camp Agudah Midwest, a religious camp in Michigan, where two vandals spray-painted a swastika and damaged a building, according to the Associated Press. That incident came two weeks after an attack at upstate New York's Camp Karlin Stolin, in which three teenagers threw bottles and coins at campers and staff. (Karlin Stolin references a Hasidic dynasty originating in Belarus.)

At Camp Seneca Lake in Honesdale, Pennsylvania, on the advice of the State Police, camp owner Irv Bader now has guards checking all trucks entering the camp for deliveries. The camp has also hired 24-hour armed security, "not rent-a-cops," Bader said, and installed a network of security cameras that are monitored around the clock. At night, the camp is illuminated with high-wattage lighting.

"It looks like daylight in the camp," Bader said.

A Camp Action Plan

The Camp Action Plan focuses on identifying potential threats and describes procedures on how to organize to spot a threat and what to do when a perceived threat appears.

Camps need to have

- a protocol for identifying a threat
- a strong policy of confronting a threat on the periphery
- law enforcement must be notified immediately, even if staff thinks the intruder was not hostile or a threat (this is not a judgment that should be made independently of law enforcement)
- in case an intruder becomes confrontational, campers should be moved to safe areas in the camp

Confronting a threat on the periphery delays the intruder's ability to penetrate the area and harm campers or staff. Delay can be accomplished with physical barriers, alert monitoring of vulnerable areas, and by the use of armed guards.

In almost all known incidents involving armed attacks against properties, the attacks generally materialize around front entrances to facilities. Thusly, synagogues are attacked through the front door, or on the steps if there are steps, or on the periphery as congregants come or go from the temple. In the case of the attack at the Washington DC Holocaust Museum, the shooter entered the building from the front door carrying a hunting rifle.

An attack launched from any spot other than the entrances of the camp cannot be ruled out. Nor can the possibility of persons "wandering" onto the camp's land area.

The recent shooting at a California Garlic Festival is a case in point where the shooter bypassed front gate security and cut through a perimeter fence that was not monitored.

An intruder may appear "innocent", but whose intention is to gather information about security conditions at the camp. The intruder may be carrying a camera or use a cell phone to make photos. In many terrorist attacks (other than purely opportunistic knife and gun attacks at popular gathering points such as bus stops), the terrorist works from information gathered about the site either by the terrorist or colleagues of the terrorist. In the United States, there are a number of reports of synagogues and community centers photographed or where "visitors" show up to assess facility security.

In the horrific attack in Norway, on 22 July 2011 on the Workers' Youth League Summer Camp, Andras Breivik dressed in a phony police uniform and carrying a fake ID card was let into the camp at its front entrance and shot and killed some 77 people, mainly campers. Earlier, Breivik had placed a bomb in a van in the government quarter in Oslo; the explosion killed 8 people and wounded 209. Even after the downtown bombing and hours before the camp shooting, the Norwegian police did not sound a nation-wide alert, although the bomber was still at large.

Recommended physical and technical improvements for camps include:

- Camera monitoring of the main entrance and the staff entrance
- Electronically controlled gates that are only opened when there is positive identification of the visitor
- An escort system for all visitors
- Controlled entrance of staff using an access control system at gates activated by a key fob or other similar device (card access)
- Where vehicles are driven onto the property, vehicles should be checked at the entrance before the gates are opened—the danger of a hijacked or fake delivery vehicle holding terrorists is a real threat

- Monitoring of areas by camera near the gates where a walk-in penetration is possible
- Cameras and motion sensors in areas that are outside the main entrances
- Armed guards on a full-time basis with appropriate uniforms and equipment
- Panic buttons located throughout the camp
- Improved lighting and motion-sensor triggered lighting
- A police scanner radio to get alerts on any local incidents
- Two-way (walkie talkie) radios for security guards and staff
- A command center in the administration building, operating full-time
- A camp-wide monitoring system consisting of a siren and siren signals that are understood by campers and staff
- A voice paging system
- A lockdown system for main buildings where camp personnel and campers can be temporarily protected (where feasible)
- A Quadrant Evacuation Plan (see below) plus approved secure buildings to protect campers and staff
- A buddy system for campers and staff
- Urgent and immediate contact with police by telephone or emergency radio
- A digital, wireless camera system for the facility integrated with motion sensors and panic buttons
- Security Signage—at all gates and around the campus

IMPORTANT: Never answer any questions from an unidentified visitor. Some "visitors" will seek to find out by probing what security is in place, what the layout of the camp is, where campers sleep and eat, who attends the camp etc.

IMPORTANT: Staff and campers should be instructed to immediately report any "strange" person they encounter anywhere in the camp. If there are panic buttons located on the campus, staff and campers should use them to summon security.

IMPORTANT: "Strange" Visitors should be denied entrance or, if found inside the security perimeter, immediately escorted off the property. If possible make a photo of the "strange" visitor and also take a photo of the visitor's vehicle's license plate.

IMPORTANT: For camps located on public grounds or property it is important to coordinate with local authorities on what security measures can legally be used. It is also a good idea to ask what security services the locality can provide (such as police services, rescue services etc.).

Quadrant Evacuation

In a camp setting, evacuation is very difficult because of the wilderness nature of the camp's location and other natural barriers (e.g., lakes and streams).

Moreover, if all campers are directed to one location it is likely an active shooter may track them to that location.

Therefore setting up quadrant evacuation overcomes some of the difficulty of a single evacuation location.

One workable idea is to divide evacuation areas into four or more locations that are reasonably accessible. Staff will need to be equipped with flashlights to guide campers if the evacuation takes place at night-time.

The quadrant system needs to be carefully tested. It is especially important to move campers far enough away from the threatened area for safety. It is also important that the evacuation area be reasonably safe and that minimal supplies are stored at these locations (such as water and snacks).

Staff should be equipped with walkie-talkie radios.

Staff Training

Camp Staff need comprehensive training and must be provided with written guidance on responsibilities and how to handle any threat.

Key staff and guards must be equipped with two-way radios with secure connections. In particular, the Incident Commander (see below) and the Rapid Response Team need to be able to communicate with the Security Guards.

Explosive Devices & Camps

Explosives are typically used by terrorists or those connected to terrorists, whether antisemitic or anti-black right wing organizations (Neo-Nazi, Ku Klux Klan) or left-wing organizations (Antifa[57]), and various terrorist organizations (e.g., al-Qaeda, ISIS).

Explosives can be made of commercially available energetic material, most typically TNT, or from military grade energetic material, particularly those materials that constitute the class of so-called Plastic Explosives such as PETN[58], RDX[59] or (when combined) Semtex[60].

Explosives can take many forms, such as Suicide Belts, tossed or thrown grenades or small bombs (with crude fuses), or explosives in containers or placed in or under vehicles.

Unknown visitors with backpacks should be kept away from any interaction with campers and handled exclusively by security personnel. If security personnel are not present when the intruder appears, security should immediately be called.

Visitors carrying satchels or wearing backpacks should be searched.

Explosives can be triggered by fuses, by timers and by remote control devices, including cell phones and garage door openers. Remotely controlled crude, homemade bombs are often referred to as IEDs (Improvised Explosive Devices).

Churches, synagogues, mosques and community centers as well as government buildings and other venues have been attacked with bombs of different kinds, some in vehicles, some on persons (backpacks, explosive vests) and others planted.

Letter bombs are also used from time to time. Packages and envelopes sometimes contain poisons or biological hazards such as Anthrax or poisons such as ricin.

Every camp must put in place a strict policy on packages mailed or delivered to the camp. While campers may receive packages from home, packages should be validated with the camper before they are opened.

Explosive packages, or packages with poisons inside are a significant danger and have been used by criminals, by terrorist groups (such as al-Qaeda) and others.

Effective Measures against Bombs at Camps

Bombs are easily concealed on persons, hidden in packages and containers, or inside or underneath vehicles.

Any unrecognized package, box, or container should be treated as a potential threat and if possible, isolated. Because package and container bombs can be "tripped" by movement, help should immediately be requested.

Packages from unrecognized addresses received by mail or delivery (i.e., FEDEX, DHL etc.) should not be opened unless the sender is known and the package expected.

Bombs can also be hidden in supplies delivered to the camp or a vehicle hijacked and stuffed with explosives entering the camp under false pretenses.

Suicide bombers will seek access to the camp, perhaps as posing as an innocent delivery person or as a law officer, or a health or safety inspector.

It is important to always demand positive identification from any visitor and wherever possible to confirm his or her organizations sent the person to the camp. While confirmation is in process the person should be kept isolated and away from campers and staff.

IMPORTANT: Delivery vehicles need to be held at the camp gate until they are verified. A simple phone call to the company sending supplies can assess whether the truck and the driver are authorized. Always ask the driver's name and call the delivery company to verify. The possibility of hijacked trucks has to be kept firmly in mind.

Training to Understand Camp Threats

Training in understanding the dangers of different types of bomb threats is very important for staff and security personnel. The threat profile for different types of bomb attacks runs in unusual and unanticipated cycles, and many attacks are copycat, meaning that if a type of attack occurs at one venue, there is a good chance it will be repeated elsewhere.

Suicide bombers, for example, usually require training and outside help and support and in some cases the suicide bomber is pumped up with drugs to bolster his or her self confidence in carrying out an assignment. Persons acting strangely or who seem to have impaired speaking could be potential suicide bombers.

Most importantly, staying aware of global threats and threat profiles and sharing of such information among security personnel and staff is a cost effective and useful step in raising awareness and alertness and in thinking ahead on means to block any bombing threat.

Other Violent Attacks in Camps

Other violent attacks with crude hand-held weapons, with knives especially, has been growing particularly in radical Islamic terrorism incidents in Israel, Europe and elsewhere.

In Israel, knife attacks by Palestinians have happened fairly frequently and knife incidents have spread to Europe. In the UK, there is a major escalation in knifing incidents, generally resulting in death if not serious injury. Most of the UK violence appears to be gang related, though some of the incidents are hate crimes and crimes aimed at minorities.

Attacks with knives, hammers, rocks, stones and such are particularly hard to control before damage is done. These attacks can come from outside, but can also come from disgruntled employees, those who are mentally deranged or other causes. A knife attack by a camper against a camper or staff person for whatever perceived grievance is another ever-present (if uncommon) danger.

Effective Measures against Violent Non-Gun Attacks in Camps

In Israel, most knife attacks are dealt with by armed intervention by police, military or sometimes bystanders. Unfortunately, most of the time the intervention is after an attack has occurred or is underway.

Defense against knife attacks using martial arts or reality-based self-defense is still controversial. Most of the time an aggressor with a knife will lead his or her attack with the empty hand out in front of the knife. Even then, often the knife is hidden from view until the attack commences.

- Knife attacks happen very fast, typically within 14 seconds. And knife attacks often include conversation contact with the individual— threats are not usually made far from the victim.

The immediate best strategy is to run away from the assailant while calling for help.

Often victims fall backwards trying to get away from the attacker. This leads to stumbling and falling, giving the assailant a chance to do harm. It is better to turn and run.

It is not a good idea for a victim to try and confront the attacker. Leave that to the security team.

- Expect people to be wounded in knife attacks. First aid and training in dealing with puncture and slash wounds is very important. Sometimes victims don't know right away they have been wounded.

Very often wounds are in the upper body torso, even the face and neck region. This would be especially the case of campers who will for the most part likely be smaller than the assailant.

Neutralizing an Attacker in Camps

Training is important for security personnel to neutralize an attacker. Training should be done by professionals who can help security staff and camp staff on how they can confront, isolate and stop a security threat.

Camps also need to train personnel in emergency medical procedures, especially means to stop bleeding, how to use tourniquets and other bandages and how to calm the victim.

Emergency triage training for key personnel is important as is having on hand adequate supplies to deal with those wounded in any confrontation.

Triage is the sorting of wounded based on the urgent need for medical attention and specific risks such as 'bleeding out.'

Security personnel should follow best practices in stopping an active knife attack[61].

Most knife attacks, other than gang related, are usually individual attacks. However, the spread of gang violence in the UK with many local thugs armed with knives, swords and other weapons (such as chains), suggests that this trend may mutate to some terrorist organizations in the US and Canada and not solely be confined to gang violence.

A typical case is that of Amor M. Ftouhi, 50, of Montreal, Canada who on June 20, 2017 walked up to Lieutenant Jeff Neville of the Bishop Airport Authority, who was in full uniform, and stabbed the police officer in the neck with a knife. Mr. Ftouhi referenced killings in Syria, Iraq and Afghanistan, and yelled "Allah Akbar." After his arrest, Mr. Ftouhi told law enforcement that he was a "soldier of Allah" and subscribed to the ideology of al-Qaeda and Usama bin Laden.

In another Canadian case, Rehab Dughmosh was convicted in February, 2019 by a jury on terrorism-related charges for two separate incidents. For the June 3, 2017 attack at a Scarborough Canadian Tire shop, a short walk from her home, she was convicted of two counts of assault with a weapon (a golf club and a knife) and one count of carrying a weapon (a bow) for a dangerous purpose. She was also convicted on one count of leaving Canada, in April 2016, to commit an offense, specifically joining ISIS.

Knife attacks can be stopped, but it is axiomatic that those who engage a knife-wielding assailant are likely to be wounded in the process.

For campers the best strategy is to train them to seek immediate help while running from an assailant.

Camps should install Alert Panic devices throughout the camp, including near buildings, paths, swimming and other sports related areas.

Kidnappings and Sexual and other Assaults in Camps

CBS News[62] "has identified hundreds of reports of sexual abuse that occurred at children's camps across the United States. [CBS] found reports of more than 500 victims who were allegedly sexually abused at children's camps over the past 55 years. At least 21 of those cases surfaced [in] (2018) alone."

CBS goes on to say "More than 14 million people attend camps each year. But there are no national regulations for camps to follow. Eight states have no requirements for overnight camps to be licensed, and 18 states don't require background checks for employees."

It goes without saying that church-run camps and profit and non-profit camps all face the same sort of problem.

Background checks on staff is very important and by no means should be neglected.

Today, camps can be held liable if they fail to take reasonable precautions against both internal and external threats that could lead to kidnappings or sexual abuse of children.

In remote areas, the danger of kidnappings and physical assaults, especially sexual assaults are a persistent threat.

Well located Alert Panic devices are an important security enhancement, but this is not enough by itself.

IMPORTANT: Camps should institute a strict buddy system for campers, so that campers do not wander off by themselves or find themselves isolated from others.

Buddy systems have long proven their value for security and accountability.

Camp personnel have to frequently check the presence of campers in all activities including meals.

Boy scouts, girl scouts, US military departments (Army, Navy, Air Force, Marines, and National Guards) all use a buddy system as a matter of policy.

The Doctrine and Covenants of the Church of Jesus Christ of Latter-day Saints states:

> "Ye shall go forth in the power of my Spirit, preaching my gospel, two by two, in my name, lifting up your voices as with the sound of a trumpet, declaring my word like unto angels of God." (Doctrine and Covenants, 42)
>
> Ecclesiastes Chapter 4 says: "Two are better than one. For if they fall, one will lift up his fellow: but woe to him that is alone when he falleth; for he hath not another to help him up."

IMPORTANT: The Buddy System works when it is strongly enforced by staff and counselors. At camp a well-enforced Buddy System is an important way to prevent dangerous incidents.

Trespassing in Camps

Trespassing can be accidental or on purpose and sometimes it is difficult to tell the reason.

All trespassing on the camp property, therefore must be treated as a threat.

When encountered, a trespasser should be ushered off the property immediately before any conversation take place.

Any filming, video or picture taking by anyone in or around the property should be regarded as trespassing.

If an individual arrives by car or truck and is immediately asked to leave, staff must write down (1) the license plate (2) the model and color of the vehicle and (3) whether there are other passengers. Even better, a photo of the individual or individuals and his/their vehicle is very useful because it can be quickly transmitted to police.

The information should immediately be passed to local law enforcement. If the security cameras are operating, the video of the recording should be copied and given immediately to law enforcement.

If the trespasser resists leaving or tries to delay leaving or asks questions, the response is only singular: the person must leave the camp area immediately. Staff and security personnel should summon additional help and immediately call police.

What Trespassers Want

The trespasser could be a criminal such as a robber or a sexual predator or a terrorist or someone engaged by criminals or terrorists to collect information.

Keep in mind that today, almost everyone has access to some overhead and ground level information about a camp because of publicly available information such as Google Maps.

Some camps have web pages with information about the camps, including directions, a diagram of the camp layout, and photos. Web sites should be carefully reviewed and security sensitive photos removed. (Camp operators should give serious consideration to removing diagrams of a camp or, if that is not possible, minimizing the amount of information portrayed on diagrams.)

Potential attackers often want to count heads and get an idea of the security set up, so they will survey the campsite, try and engage staff and campers in conversation to get information, and either openly or surreptitiously take pictures or record video.

There are very few terrorist incidents that occur without some form of surveillance preceding the attack.

Keep in mind that surveillance on a property can take places weeks, months or even years before a security incident occurs. Or nothing will happen when other more suitable targets are found or for other reasons an attack does not occur.

If there is a camera system at the camp, video should be regularly reviewed to detect intruders that may have been at the camp, such as in off-season. Most modern camera systems can record many days of activities and where to look in saved video can be enhanced by other sensors such as motion detectors that will report a possible intrusion based on date and time, making video review easier.

It is absolutely vital that camp staff and campers not give out any information whatever about the camp.

Reporting

It is very important to always report an incident to local law enforcement and to ask local law enforcement to check with the FBI or other national law enforcement organization if they know of any active threats against certain groups, individuals or camps.

This all-important rule often isn't followed and camp managers or employees tend to dismiss the appearance of a trespasser and don't follow up.

In fact, "small" camp incidents such as thefts or minor incidents are not reported because a camp may not want to advertise problems that could impact its subscribers and supporters.

Camps need to adopt a policy of reporting all incidents, small or large to local law enforcement.

IMPORTANT: It is vital that any trespassing incident is immediately reported to authorities. No exceptions!

Remote Camp Organization

All remotely located camps need security guards who are competent and professional.

The same issues on whether guards should be armed discussed in the prior chapters is in play when it comes to summer camps, particularly those in remote locations where summoning help may take much longer than in urban and suburban communities that have nearby police stations or substations. In rural areas, it could take between 15 minutes to 30 minutes before a police cruiser can arrive if summoned.

Camps need to be actively patrolled around the clock and every day when campers are present.

Guards should also keep watch on the camp grounds when the camp itself is idle.

Camera systems and sensors should be continuously monitored during camp sessions and off-time, to see if there are any intruders and what they are doing at the site. Police need to be called even during off-time when there are intruders.

Remote camps also need to develop a liaison relationship with local law enforcement, fire brigades and first responders.

Camp management needs to understand how long it would take for help to arrive and to plan accordingly.

Chain of Command in Camps

It is critical to establish a Chain of Command for every camp with defined responsibilities.

A camp should establish a Command Center that has communications, access to security systems, and is the focus for necessary security coordination.

Incident Commander(s): A designated employee or group of employees who is/are responsible for taking immediate action on site, including sounding alarms and organizing the use of life-saving equipment and firefighting equipment, immediately notifying First Responders (police, fire brigades and ambulance services) and properly training staff on procedures to minimize casualties, provide triage to injured persons, and support to First Responders.

The Incident Commander needs to be trained in his/her responsibilities and requires support people on and off site.

Support staff must also be trained and the entire on-site crew needs to practice against different types of emergencies, including evacuation of the buildings and at-risk outside areas.

Rapid Response team: An Incident Commander needs a backup in case of absence or otherwise unavailable.

A Rapid Response Team should be created to coordinate with the Incident Commander or when the Commander is missing, replace the Incident Commander. The Team should place at least one person in the camp's Command Center and at least one other outside focusing on the threat.

The Rapid Response Team when the Incident Commander is available should train to work with the Incident Commander both by providing intelligence on any threat and helping to implement the Camp Action Plan.

Security Team: A full-time Security Team with appropriate shifts is needed. The Security Team works at the direction of the Incident Commander, but must be authorized to implement a response to a threat immediately without prior coordination.

The Security Team needs proper equipment, immediately recognizable uniforms, and two-way secure communications.

Whether armed or not, Security Team personnel should wear protective clothing. Security team members should carry radios, alert sounding devices, batons and high-powered flashlights for night work. Security team members may also carry some emergency triage gear, such as bandages.

When there is a security team and hired guards, team members and guards should carefully work out the duties and responsibilities each has to avoid overlaps and confusion.

When good organization is lacking and where staff have little or no training, the ability to respond efficiently and professionally is at risk.

Security at Day Camps

There are many day camps, some directly affiliated with churches, mosques, temples and synagogues, others with a religious orientation such as the YMCA. The YMCA is a worldwide organization with more than 58 million participants from 125 national associations. It was founded on 6 June 1844 in London and aims to put Christian principles into practice by developing a healthy "body, mind and spirit". The YMCA offers summer camping, including day camps in many towns and cities.

Day camps differ in some respects from overnight camps because they generally use community facilities such as public parks and playgrounds and community centers. Many day camps are also located at churches, synagogues, mosques and temples and use their classrooms, social halls, gyms and playgrounds.

Most of the rules for overnight camps apply equally to day camps, but day camps rarely have dedicated security staff and typically are run by teachers and counselors who are working a summer job.

Protecting day-campers from harm is a challenge often because of the lack of security and a limited staff working part time.

When campers are indoors as in a church site, then the existing security protocols should be used. To make this work the camp leaders need to coordinate with the church to assure that security systems are working and to work out ways to best protect campers indoors. Many use armed security guards the same way as they would for religious services.

When campers are indoors and if a threat is detected, lock down procedures should be used.

When campers are outdoors and in fenced areas, staff should be trained to move them indoors in case there is any perceived threat.

Many play areas are fenced in, but this is not always the case.

With young campers intensive adult supervision is needed.

Summer-time day camp personnel have to be extremely careful about the dropping off and picking up of campers from the camp, assuring that campers get in a vehicle with a responsible, well-known adult. It is best to allow pick-ups by an authorized person unless the camp is notified in advance by the authorized person of an emergency change in pick-up responsibility. In this last case, care should be taken to make sure that the "authorized person" calling is in fact the person who really is authorized. Checking a phone number, calling back to verify and similar authenticating steps are very important to avert a tragedy.

IMPORTANT: For day camps in public spaces, check with your municipal authorities on what security measures are permitted. Also ask what services the municipality can offer to enhance security.

CHAPTER 7

Security Technology

S ecurity technology is evolving rapidly after having been stagnant for many years. Take, as an example burglar alarms that are used commercially and in homes.

Old home alarms and also those used in commercial sites used to require copper wires with magnetic sensors placed at every window and door, all of which had to be installed and wired to a central control box. If you wanted a motion detector these often were lensed infrared lights, with a transmitting and receiving station. If an intruder "broke the light beam" an alarm would trigger. The entire system worked using the electrical power of the building, meaning that if power was lost, the alarm system would stop working too.

Old alarms would set off a siren or bell to alert the community. Some also would signal an alarm company who would then summon police.

Today, alarm systems have changed as technology evolved. Alarms now work on batteries backed up by house electrical power; they can automatically dial a security company who will alert police, using either a land line, cellular connection or Wi-Fi. These systems can turn on lighting, pick up intruders using motion sensors, and "hear" a door or window being smashed thanks to breakage sensors. Moreover, modern alarm systems are wireless, so the sensor can communicate with the alarm system using built in radio communications. Sensors also have their own batteries.

Alarm systems can also trigger cameras and camera images can be viewed remotely in real time, and can be transmitted securely using the Internet.

Like burglar alarms, other security equipment has also evolved.

Let's take a look at what is out there and what will soon appear in the market.

Camera Systems

Cameras can provide coverage inside and outside a building. Older cameras were analog and the camera image was the same as an old TV, fairly low resolution. Many of these older cameras are still in use (and sometimes their analog output is converted to a digital format to work with computers). But digital cameras and modern software have been replacing analog systems everywhere because they are far less expensive, easier to maintain and offer much better picture quality.

Digital Cameras

The advantages of a modern digital camera include much higher image resolution and a host of special features that combine optical imagery and digital enhancement. Digital cameras often have image zoom capability that makes it possible to focus on the face of an intruder or the license plate of a car.

Older Analog Security Cameras (Hustvedt CC-BY-SA 3.0)

Images from a digital camera can easily be transmitted over Wi-Fi or through the Internet, and modern digital cameras often are connected to the main security system through Wi-Fi, meaning that the only wiring they need is for electrical power. The better cameras also include rechargeable batteries, so if power is lost the cameras will continue to work. Power backup systems are also available for servers and Wi-Fi systems that support the camera network. Some cameras also can illuminate a target at night, or have dual daylight and infrared capability.

Wireless Security Camera (by FDT)

Digital camera systems can be enhanced with different kinds of software, such as facial recognition or by a moving target designator. Camera images can also incorporate automatic license plate reading software, which is now available in the market. While not perfect in reading license plate information, it provides important forensic information to law enforcement.

WARNING: Not all digital cameras are secure if they are connected to Wi-Fi or to the Internet or both. There is increasing concern about cameras that have electronic "back doors" that allow outsiders to view imagery generated by cameras. In cases where professional terrorists or hackers have access to camera surveillance systems, either they can use that information themselves or sell or trade it. It is strongly recommended to check if your camera system comes from a reliable source, and not to use cameras that are considered vulnerable to hacking. Similarly it is important to place cameras only in places where compromises of personal privacy can be avoided.

Today's cameras are relatively inexpensive and modern software to control them can allow for the use of a relatively large number of cameras. In short, the better systems are scalable.

Most camera systems also include recording and video storage so that information from the cameras can be used by the security staff and law enforcement.

Face Recognition

Face recognition systems are growing in popularity, although some jurisdictions are beginning to question their intrusiveness. But they offer an excellent chance to input pictures of known threats and to sound an alarm when a camera detects one.

Modern video surveillance systems can be bought with face recognition software that can support a database of faces, including "friendly" and "unfriendly" and can sound alarms when it detects an unknown or known "unfriendly" visitor.

As the resolution of outdoor and indoor cameras continues to improve, the viability of highly accurate facial recognition grows. Today's commercial surveillance cameras offer up to 20 megapixel resolution and use high quality professional camera lenses.

New technology is also coming on stream with camera systems that can see clearly even in bad weather, such as fog, rain or snow. This is done by means of sophisticated algorithms that removes "noise" from the image, rendering a far clearer and accurate result. As cameras continue to improve in hardware, firmware and software, the cost of camera systems continues to go down. This makes it relatively easy and cost-effective to upgrade or expand existing systems.

Face recognition systems vary in how they work and the level of accuracy they provide, which is usually judged by the likelihood of recognizing a face and by how many false positives are generated. All of them are based on biometric algorithms that detect certain features and/or measure spaces between features (e.g. space between eyes and space between tip of nose and mouth) and check images to see how they compare to stored biometric information. Be Aware that smart intruders will wear dark glasses to try and obscure their face, so don't rely on face recognition systems to work perfectly. Maybe you have been asked at TSA check spots at airports to remove your hat or sunglasses. This is ostensibly for checking your photo on your driver's license or passport, but it may also be done in connection with face recognition cameras you don't see.

In the not too far future, it will be possible to plug video surveillance systems into live police or law enforcement photo imagery data sources, making it possible to identify a threat through linking to law enforcement databases.

License Plate Readers

License plate reader hardware and software can either be built into security cameras or work in conjunction with standard security cameras if the cameras are properly positioned and have adequate image resolution. Most cameras sold today are good enough to perform the license plate reading mission. Some have long range lenses and the ability to operate at night as well as during the day.

License Plate Reader Security Camera with Night Vision and Long Range Lens (by HDView)

A license plate reader (or "number plate" outside of the United States) basically takes an image of a license plate and optically scans it to extract the numbers and letters on the plate, essentially converting an image into machine-readable characters. This is a complex task because license plates vary by state, often have half-size characters and sometimes graphics that intrude on the image. Many auto owners also are known to put colored plastic over their license plates to defeat police license plate scanners. But increasingly sophisticated matching systems that can even invert images or otherwise manipulate them to make them more readily scanable are found in high-end automatic license plate reading systems.

TAKE NOTE: If vehicles are seen around your holy place with obscured or suspicious license plates, report that information to the police. If possible write down the number information and state shown on the license plate.

A license plate reader can perform different functions. It can detect approved number plates of congregation members and it can pick out number plates that are not on an approved list. Staff can enter suspect license plate numbers provided by law enforcement into your camera software database, which will trigger an alarm if the cameras detects them.

In future and depending on legal requirements, license plate reading cameras in private hands may be networked into law enforcement systems.

Artificial Intelligence (AI) Cameras

Artificial intelligence is either being built into cameras or can be added to existing cameras in a network. The idea is to create smart cameras that can perform security tasks, even in a sense to act as virtual guards.

The key technology for an AI-enabled camera is called behavioral analytics. A camera can either be taught or can self-learn "normal" behavior patterns, and it can alert security personnel if there is an out-of-normal behavior detected. Cameras can learn the behavior of individuals, groups of individuals and normal and non-normal patterns for vehicles. When an abnormal behavior is detected, some AI cameras not only send alerts but track the apparent intruder.

One simple and well developed technology that partially falls into the AI category is a "virtual fence." A virtual fence is a marked off area around a facility or even inside a facility. If the virtual fence is crossed, the security operator is alerted and the image of the person or persons crossing the virtual fence is highlighted and tracked. Someone entering a school yard when the entrance gates are closed is one use of a virtual fence. (It can also be used of course to sound an alert if a child leaves the premises without permission.)

A virtual fence exists only in your camera software and is defined by the security staff. It can be changed or modified to suit security needs.

Some AI technologies can recognize a gun or other weapon and immediate broadcast a high security alert and pinpoint and track the person or persons with a gun. This provides security personnel and law enforcement with excellent situational awareness on the location and movements of an active shooter, or potential shooter. Smart gun recognition technology keeps evolving and readers are encouraged to see what the market is offering. This is an exciting area that can augment security meaningfully.

There is increasing interest in networking AI-supported camera systems such as linking security systems at religious sites to police. While some oppose the idea for reasons of privacy, in sensitive locations police access to potential threats could prove to be life-saving.

AI enabled systems work with other technologies including facial recognition. For example, a known threat's image or a particular vehicle can be programmed into an AI system and will raise an alarm if that person or vehicle is detected.

Many schools in the United States and governments both in the US, Canada, the UK, Australia and elsewhere are adopting AI-enabled systems.

This is a rapidly evolving technology space because AI technology itself is cutting edge and new capabilities are rapidly emerging.

Holy Places can certainly make use of AI-enabled camera systems, but should keep in mind the following:

- be careful what system you choose and make sure it performs up to your requirements, not the claimed capabilities of the vendor;
- do not rely on AI as a way to reduce the number of security personnel protecting a location. AI is a supplement but does not replace live security guards.

Gunshot Detection

Wireless security systems often have microphones built in, which can perform a variety of tasks.

One of those tasks is gunshot detection.

Security guards who may be inside a building may not hear a gunshot outside and not know a security incident has taken place. This is especially important where there are remote buildings or large parking areas.

Sometimes it is not possible to tell the difference between a gunshot and a vehicle that backfires. And, criminals and terrorists have access to gun sound suppressors ("silencers") that reduce the sound of a gun discharge.

Gunshot detection can be integrated into camera systems with specialized software.

One company called Surveillance Secure[63] says its software can be used on existing camera surveillance systems (equipped with microphones). The company has worked with churches and religion-based schools primarily in and around Maryland.

The advantage of this software is that it will immediately notify guards and security personnel that a gun has been fired and where the threat was when it was fired (what camera picked up the shooting). This means guards won't be blindsided or respond too late to a developing security crisis.

For faith-based institutions adding a gunshot detection feature to an existing camera system is a sensible step. It is especially useful for remote parking lots and locations around a large campus. But even in a city center, a gunshot detector can immediately alert security personnel who can either investigate the shooting or summon police. The more sophisticated gunshot detection systems use multiple microphone arrays so they can pinpoint the location of the shooter.

Panic Alert Systems

The security company Kintronics[64] says that "Panic buttons can be added to security systems to increase safety and security. For example, these alarm buttons can be integrated into a security system such as surveillance camera systems, paging systems, and door access control systems. Placing panic buttons in strategic areas can help to assure quick response to emergencies. There is even a mobile personal panic button that can be carried with you."

Here is what Kintronics says about adding Panic Alert to camera systems:

"Many network-attached surveillance cameras have I/O [Input, Output] connections. The button can be attached to the I/O input to provide a signal to the video management software. The alert appears on the security person's console, along with the video from a nearby camera.

"Once the security person is notified of the emergency, they can determine the best course of action. The surveillance camera system provides the information they need to make a decision.

"It is important to use video management software that includes the ability to notify the security person"

Panic alerts can also be added to paging systems and to intercoms.

Panic alert buttons are important to have at the guard desk or in the hands of the guards to trigger a public address announcement in case of an emergency. Such a system buys vital time for congregants and staff to take action, such as locking access doors, classroom doors or, if necessary evacuation.

Wireless campus panic buttons can provide a means for calling help from any location, inside and outside of buildings, in parking lots and outbuildings. These campus-wide type panic devices are battery powered and wireless. Hard wired versions also are available.

These devices can be integrated into a comprehensive security system.

The key to any panic button alert system is for the alert to be clearly and visibly marked, easy to access and supported by good lighting and sirens or other equipment designed to spook anyone trying to attack or harm a congregant or visitor.

Many security companies can integrate these features into existing security systems, or upgrade security systems to support these capabilities.

Emergency call boxes are also very effective and are ideal for large campuses. Today they are often found on college campuses, but can be just as easily adopted for schools and churches, particularly with large open areas with roads and parking areas.

Emergency Call Box with Alarm Button (by Case Emergency Systems)

Lighting and Sirens

Outdoor Lighting

KEEP IN MIND: Good lighting is a powerful deterrent to crime, especially around the perimeter of a building and in parking areas and other "dark" spots where a threat could be lurking.

Modern systems can either run full-time (dusk to dawn) or be triggered by a motion sensor. Top quality motion sensors will pick up any movement and can also trigger camera activity and alarms.

LED pole lights are a popular choice because they are reasonably energy efficient. LED Pole Lights can be used as street lights in parking lots and also provide good visibility for drivers entering or leaving parking areas and roadways by illuminating pedestrians and other vehicles.

Flood lights are another popular option and though there are energy efficient floodlights on the market, buyers need to check light output to make sure the illumination covers important areas. LED floodlights are available, some operating at over 600 watts and producing 96,000 lumens output.

LED lights are more energy efficient than metal halide or fluorescent fixtures and last much longer. Halogen bulbs burn out after around 1,000 hours. Incandescent lamps might make it to 2,000 hours. Fluorescent tubes and compact fluorescent lights burn out after 7,000 to 15,000 hours while LED lights can last between 30,000 to 130,000 hours, depending to some degree on design and materials and on the outside environment. LED lamps also don't lose luminescence over time.

Outdoor lighting can also be solar powered, but only the highest power solar lighting would be appropriate for security. The real benefit of both solar powered and battery powered lighting is that it works when there is a power outage. Solar powered lighting, however does not appear to have the output needed for good security and probably is best only for backup.

Indoor Security Lighting

Indoor security lighting is very important if, for any reason, there is a power outage.

Power can fail for many reasons: a short circuit or other fault at a facility; a fire or other problem that can shut down lighting; bad weather (lightening) disrupting city-supplied electrical power; a major power failure in the grid; or tampering with outside power.

For holy places located in rural areas, particularly in zones where power outages are fairly common, backup generators should be considered as an option. Alternatively, back up solar-powered electrical systems can support building and outside lighting.

A typical indoor product may combine LED flood bulbs with battery backup. Some use lithium batteries, others use cadmium batteries. These lights typically operate for between one and two hours solely on battery power when there is a city-power failure or faulty electrical system.

It is important to have good coverage for security lighting, which often is overlooked. For example, stairs and exit areas should have good security lighting and there also should be outdoor security lighting in support of emergency evacuations. Consideration should also be given to flush floor lamps to direct evacuation, similar to the lighting used on floors in aircraft for emergencies.

Computer and Security Battery Backup Systems

It is important to keep security systems functioning if there is a power failure.

Battery backup products are available to keep computer servers going, and surveillance cameras are also available that have built- in backup batteries.

Backup batteries can also be used for public address systems and for panic button systems.

It is important to get professional advice on backing up security systems which can be done either by rechargeable battery packs designed for that purpose, or by backup generators that support lighting and security systems. Generators can be either natural gas ("city gas") or fueled by LNG (liquefied natural gas), otherwise called propane. Large enough storage bottles are available to run a generator for either hours or days.

Sirens and Alarms

There are a wide variety of sirens and alarms, some with wireless connections to the security system, others hard wired.

Some sirens combine remote controls and can also trigger an LED flasher, a useful feature to help ward off intruders. The remote control offers a good feature to turn off an alarm if it was tripped inadvertently or by an animal.

For a large campus, the outside alarm or alarms should be loud enough so that guards inside the building can hear them.

Some outdoor and indoor alarms can be triggered by motion detection, by glass break sensors or by audible screams for help, or triggered by panic buttons.

Indoors it is important to have very distinct alarm sounds to distinguish between a fire and a security threat.

For fire, a bell or buzzer style alarm is best. For security, a horn blasting sound is clearly different from a bell or buzzer.

In a security event inside, there is very little time and a lockdown alert needs to be clearly understood by teachers, staff and congregational leaders.

In the past, alarms typically depended either on a single sensor (smoke alarm, for example) or by activating a fire alarm box.

A modern fire alarm with built in strobe light (by SpectrAlert Advance)

Some fire alarms sound an alarm and have a built-in strobe light, as the one above that can be placed in every room, in hallways, on stairs, restrooms and other parts of the facility. They can also be installed outside if desired. The strobe light alerts deaf people.

Fire alarm pull boxes should be located throughout the interior and on the exterior of the building if the location is reasonably safe from vandalism.

A fire alert pull box that sets off an alarm and alerts the fire department (by NAPCO)

Fire alarms should connect directly to a fire brigade or a firefighting substation. In older buildings fire alarms only sounded a bell or horn but did not send any signal to firefighters. Fire marshals can advise on how to connect an alarm box to their system or alternatively through an alarm service.

Modern office buildings also have sophisticated fire control systems that indicate in a large complex where there is a fire emergency. In large religious campuses this may be a good solution. Installation of fire control systems must conform to local codes and meet local and Federal standards.

Fire extinguishers also need to be located strategically inside a building and should be accessible.

The location of outdoor fire hydrants should be clearly marked on diagrams in the building accessible to firemen and women.

A fire can sometimes be associated with a security event and planning for that eventuality is important. For example, a bomb could cause a serious fire.

Communications with Law Enforcement

One of the advantages of having off-duty police as security guards is that they can bring with them their police radios and communicate directly with the police.

Other guard-for-hire service and alarm companies generally provide an external service that is tied into the alarm system or which the guards can access either by voice communications or by a triggering switch or button.

IMPORTANT: Volunteers and staff should carry mobile phones and contact 911 (or other emergency number) unless the local police supply a direct call number for an emergency.

CHAPTER 8

Getting Outside Help

P rofessional outside help is needed in designing a security system, acquiring equipment and installing it properly, arranging training for personnel and finding ways and means to finance security improvements and pay the cost of security guards and staff.

Security Guards–Licensing

Most states require security guards to be licensed[65] and most require them to be trained either at a training establishment, on the job or both. Rules differ outside the United States and should be carefully checked.

Security guard training programs often must be completed during the first 100 days on the job, though this requirement varies by state. Topics covered during the training programs include basic security techniques, investigations, report writing, patrolling tactics, firearm use and emergency procedures. Workers specializing in particular types of security management such as private, airport, armored car or armed escort, may need to take additional courses to learn the necessary skills for these specialty security professions.

Requirements for Security Guards (U.S. Bureau of Labor Statistics)

- Required Education: High School diploma or equivalent.
- Other Requirements: On the job training and/or state mandated training programs; registration, especially for armed guards, is usually

required. 18 years of age or older; background check, fingerprint, and possibly a physical fitness test.
- Licensure/Certification: Licensure required in most states.
- Mean Salary: $28,460.

Some states have an individual credentialing process[66] for armed, security guards and an individual credentialing process for unarmed, security guards while other states credential both.

It is important to recognize that licensure is not the same as regulation. Some states set standards for security guards, but expect the employer to be responsible for their hire to meet those state standards.

Most security companies that offer guard services (armed and unarmed) also are state licensed or, certain other jurisdictions may require city, town or county (or Parish) certification.

For example, in Maryland, the law says "a person shall be licensed by the Maryland State Police as a security guard agency before the person may:
- conduct a business that provides security guard services in the State; and
- solicit to engage in a business that provides security guard services in the State
- both an individual and firm may qualify to be licensed as a security guard agency.

Some companies specifically hire off-duty police for security guards. Many police departments will promote the use of their police for special events and as guards when off-duty. Often local police offering such service will suggest a salary level but others encourage congregations to contract directly with off-duty police officers.

Outside of directly hiring off-duty police, there are companies that employ off-duty police and act as the contracting agency. One of them is called Off-duty Officers Inc.[67] which is a nation-wide company. Other security companies also try and employ off-duty police because they are usually highly experienced and regarded as reliable.

The one problem in using off-duty police is that their first obligation is to their police department, and off-duty police may be summoned by the police department at any time, making them unavailable as security guards.

Because of the possibility of being called to active duty, a backup is needed to assure continuity of security protection.

An alternative to off-duty police are retired police or retired military, particularly military who served as military police, for example the Military Police Corps/Office of the Provost Marshal General—United States Army, the Marine Corps Criminal Investigation Division (CID) or the Coast Guard Investigative Service (CGIS)

Keep in mind that retired military can make excellent guards, but retired military may need additional training.

Off-duty police, retired police, retired military especially military police are often far more experienced than security guards who qualify based on state license requirements but have never served in a law enforcement or military police capacity.

Also bear in mind that direct hires through local police departments often is less costly than hiring through any agency, since the agency naturally adds its own charges and costs onto the hourly price. On the other hand, the agency takes responsibility for the performance of its employees and also may be liable in cases of failure to perform or other problems.

The average pay for a Security Guard in the United States is $12.68 per hour. Most security guards are hired on a part time basis, but full-time hires make sense where continuous coverage is needed and Is affordable. The hourly cost will be higher in highly urban areas or where the cost of living is higher. Also remember that religious services are often on weekends when hourly pay is higher than weekly hourly rates.

Security Guards can expect an average compensation of $26,400 every year. Security Guards are paid the highest in Louisiana, where they earn an average job salary of approximately $40,120. Full-time security guards may incur benefits costs such as health insurance, retirement and social security contributions.

There are many different categories[68] of security personnel and pay varies depending on the level of expertise and years of experience.

Security Guard Contracts

Congregations hiring professional security guards need to enter into written contracts with each guard if hired individually or with the guard service if hired through a security guard company.

Of particular importance is that any contract should include a detailed explanation of the guard's responsibilities that covers both overall tasks and specific work that is expected when the guard is on duty. Prospective guards or companies engaged in providing such services should sign a confidentiality agreement that protects the religious organization and its congregants.

The firm Upcounsel™ provides[69] the following guidance which applies to security guard companies and can be adapted for individual hires:

Review the agency's license. Any legitimate contract guard agency should be more than happy to provide a copy of their business license. Once it's provided, contact your state agency that deals with licenses to validate it. You can also get a Dun & Bradstreet report to ensure the company's solvency

Get a Certificate of Liability Insurance[70]. This is so you can lay out your company's requirements for contractors insofar as employer's liability, excess liability, general liability, and workers' compensation is concerned. Such requirements should be non-negotiable, and ideally allow you to be included on the contractor's insurance policy so that you can file a claim against it, if necessary

Insert a Defense and Indemnification Clause. Sometimes referred to as "hold harmless" language, such a clause is meant to secure your business from legal actions stemming from negligence on the part of the guard contractor. If such legal action does occur, it will be the guard company that is liable, not you

Important Security Agreement Provisions

Any properly drawn security contract should have the following provisions in it:

- **Parties to the Agreement.** In this provision, the names of the parties engaged in the contract are set forth
- **Services.** Here is set out what kind of security service will be given, such as patrol, executive protection, or building security
- **Time of Completion.** This indicates the time in which the security services will take place and if those services will be for one time only or on an ongoing basis
- **Equipment.** This will indicate what equipment will be provided by both parties
- **Firearms.** This will indicate if firearms are to be included as part of security, and if so, what kinds
- **Payment and Other Expenses.** This will specify what the payment for services, reimbursement policy, and other expenses will be

Upcounsel also provides sample contracts and can assist in providing competent attorneys to draw up service contracts. This is particularly important because religious organizations often do not use formal contracting and work informally, not a good idea given the real chance that any incident may trigger legal actions against the church or religious body for malfeasance, liability or not exercising duty of care.

Upcounsel is a commercial company that provides free legal documents and provides other services for its clients.

IMPORTANT: Congregations should ask their own attorneys about the best form for contracts for guards and other employees or engage outside legal advice like that offered by Upcounsel.

Vulnerability Assessments

Every church, synagogue, mosque or temple should get a professional vulnerability assessment by an independent group or specialist.

All vulnerability assessments are based on defined risk and the degree of exposure to those risks.

A private company called Peace of Mind Technologies[71] proposes the following general outline for a vulnerability study:

Assessing Your Building's Architecture

The following questions are intended to uncover security weaknesses related to the architectural elements inside and outside your facility:

- What major structures surround your facility?
- Is your facility equipped with perimeter security in the form of fences or other barriers?
- Where are your facility's main access points and what secondary access points exist?
- Does the outside of your facility contain anti-ram devices?
- Does the parking lot and site circulation contain barriers against high-speed approaches or reductions of speed?
- Does the outside of your site contain objects that might be used as hiding places?
- Do the inside and outside of your facility contain Crime Prevention Through Environmental Design[72] (CPTED) elements?
- Do entrances and exits require significant queuing due to design or visitor management procedures?
- What critical assets are located near the main entrances or other entry points of parking lots, parking garages, loading docks or other areas? Are these critical assets protected from public areas?
- Do interior barriers create levels of security inside your building?

Assessing Your Building's Security Equipment

The following questions are intended to uncover opportunities to use your security technology more effectively:

- Do your CCTV cameras provide high resolution in low light, and are they monitored and recorded 24 hours a day, 7 days a week? How long do they record? Who monitors the recordings? Are the recordings analog or digital? Can they be viewed remotely from all devices?
- Are your surveillance cameras capable of detecting motion and proactively alerting you to potential threats? Are they integrated with your other security solutions onsite (i.e. access control system, alarm, etc.)?
- Do your cameras possess zoom capabilities with clarity? What added specifications are necessary for monitoring and assessing threats via video?
- Does your building contain an intercom system to be used throughout the facility? Is it IP-based? Can it function through your PDA [Personal Digital Assistance] devices?
- What type of hardware is used on doors and other entry portals throughout your facility? Does your access control system provide lockdown functionality?
- Are you equipped with a reporting system to generate specific, detailed data on security incidents? Are these reports generated automatically? Is there mustering?
- Are security guards able to conduct virtual tours of your facility?
- Are your security technologies integrated and monitored through a centralized platform?
- Do your security technologies operate through their own cabling and wiring, or do they use your existing network infrastructure? Is there a wireless component?
- What backup power supply is in place for all security technology?

Note that this assessment is focused on perimeter security. But interior security is equally important.

An interior assessment includes:

- The layout of the facility
- Whether there are firebreaks that would delay an armed intruder
- Where guard stations are located
- What kind of communications exist
- If there is a comprehensive security system or is one needed?
- Can classrooms and meeting rooms be locked down?
- Can the main sanctuary by locked down?
- Can the sanctuary, social hall or other parts of the facility be evacuated?
- Is there an evacuation plan?
- Is there an existing security plan in place?
- How often the plan (if existing) is reviewed?
- How frequently is the integrity of the security infrastructure checked for sound operation?
- Where are panic buttons located?
- Is there a public address system?
- Is there a fire alarm?
- Is there a warning siren?
- Is there a coherent security organization?
- Are there security guards (full-time, part time, armed, unarmed, trained, and untrained)?
- Are there supplementary security volunteers to help patrol the space?
- Is there an access control system?
- Is the staff trained in security and managing a security system?
- Are there ample medical supplies (triage, defibrillators, stretchers, blankets)?
- Is there satisfactory emergency lighting?
- Is there a school or other facility (day care, senior facility, and living quarters) that are part of the campus and are they secure?

In addition to answering all these questions, the system would need to be thoroughly tested in a professional vulnerability assessment. Outside experts should assist in conducting both the assessment and the operational testing, and help should be sought from the local Fire Marshal and from police and FBI.

It is a good idea to have separation between who does the vulnerability analysis and who actually is called on to implement the security recommendations.

IMPORTANT: The vulnerability analytics should be done by an independent expert or contractor not associated with a vendor selling equipment or providing services.

Where remediation involves many components (camera systems, alarms, barriers, gates, fences, lighting etc.) an organization may want a general security contractor and subcontractors to carry out specific tasks. In choosing technology, it is important to consider alternative suppliers, pricing, and how well the proposed solution will integrate into the overall security system and support the Security Plan.

Certification of Security Providers

ASIS International (formerly the American Association of Industrial Security) offers a number of certifications for security professionals. For example the ASIS Physical Security Professional (PSP) certification evaluates a candidate's knowledge in physical security assessments, application, design, and integration of physical security systems, and implementation of security measures.

For candidates to be eligible for the PSP certification they must have:

- Four years of progressive experience in the **physical security**[73] field.

And

- Bachelor degree or higher from an accredited institution of higher education
  Or
- Six years of progressive experience in the **physical security** field
  And
- A high school diploma, GED equivalent, or associate degree
  And
- Be employed full-time in a security-related role
- Not have been convicted of any criminal offense that would reflect negatively on the security profession, ASIS, or the certification program
- Sign and agree to abide by the **ASIS Certification Code of Conduct**[74]
- Agree to abide by the policies of the ASIS Certification programs as outlined in the [ASIS] **Certification Handbook**[75].

The Total Security Daily Advisor[76] writes: "The American Board for Certification in Homeland Security[77] offers 15 different board certifications in topics related to sensitive security information, disaster preparedness, homeland security (with five different levels of expertise), intelligence analysis, chaplaincy, national threat analysis, emergency medical response, aviation security, cyberwarfare, dignitary and executive protection, and information assurance.

"A relatively new designation was created by the Association of Threat Assessment Professionals (ATAP)[78] to demonstrate expertise in the emerging field of threat assessment and management. The Certified Threat Manager (CTM) designation requires membership in ATAP, a challenging exam, recommendations by ATAP peers, and regular recertification."

Many colleges and universities are today offering undergraduate and graduate degrees for security professionals. While many focus mostly on cyber security, there are homeland security courses that cover topics such as how to conduct a vulnerability assessment. Some of these programs are available online, such as one at Penn State[79].

The Global Society of Homeland and National Security Professionals[80] has a Homeland Certification Board. "The **Certification Board** that consists of recognized leaders in the Homeland Protection Arena. Board members include law enforcement leaders, private industry security professionals, homeland security leadership, fire service leadership, emergency management leadership, and health and medical professionals. The certification board reviews all **Certified Homeland Security Professional** requirements and ensures that they meet the highest standard. The Board Certification provides an objective means of distinguishing highly-competent homeland-protection professionals from their less experienced peers."

FEMA offers free training for faith-based organizations. Among the available training offerings are:

- Community Emergency Response Team Training
- You Are The Help Until Help Arrives Training
- FEMA's Emergency Management Institute Independent Study Course List
- IS-360: Preparing for Mass Casualty Incidents: A Guide for Schools, Higher Education, and Houses of Worship
- S-366: Planning for the Needs of Children in Disasters
- IS-368: Including People With Disabilities & Others With Access & Functional Needs in Disaster Operations
- IS-650.a: Building Partnerships with Tribal Governments
- IS-906: Workplace Security Awareness Course
- IS-907: Active Shooter: What You Can Do
- IS-909 - Community Preparedness: Implementing Simple Activities for Everyone
- IS-914: Surveillance Awareness: What You Can Do
- FEMA Voluntary Agency Training Resource Page

In purchasing security services it is always wise to inquire if the company or individuals in it are qualified and have individual certifications, whether the company is licensed in the state, and to request references (particularly for faith-based organizations).

It is also useful to check with those in the religious community who may be able to offer additional guidance and support.

The Evangelical Lutheran Church offers advice on threats and vulnerabilities on its website[81].

Catholic Mutual Group[82] offers an active shooter training scenario and training geared for its schools. This information could also be useful to construct your plan for the church and other parish buildings. You may access this training on the CMG Connect platform[83]. Also see a CARES document called "Active Shooter Emergency Response."[84] Click Member Login, enter your Username and Password, Select the Risk Management Info icon, Property, and then Emergency Preparedness.

Another helpful tool to utilize is Catholic Mutual's "Emergency Response Procedures App" for cell phones and tablets.[85] The instructions to download this app can be obtained from previous correspondence with your Arch/diocese and/ or by contacting your Claims/Risk Manager or Loss Control Representative.

Protect My Ministry[86] is an organization that offers a range of background checks for staff, guards and volunteers. The organization also offers child safety training.

CAIR offers a manual[87] on Best Practices for Mosque and Community Security.

Jewish organizations have set up a national homeland security initiative called the Secure Community Network[88] (SCN) of the Jewish Federations of North America & the Conference of Presidents of Major American Jewish Organizations. SCN was recognized as a model system for nationwide, faith-based organizations by the Department of Homeland Security.

The Community Security Service[89] (CSS) is a security nonprofit that trains volunteers and synagogue and community center staffs. CSS proactively protects the people, institutions and events of the American Jewish community. CSS safeguards the community by training volunteers in professional security techniques, providing physical security and raising public awareness about safety issues.

CHAPTER 9

Financial Assistance

Houses of worship are beginning to take security more seriously as recent attacks on churches, synagogues, mosques and temples have raised the level of concern nationwide in the United States, as it has in many other countries.

This means reaching into tight budgets to try and support needed security improvements and pay for security guards.

With attendance at many churches and synagogues in a downward spiral, finding adequate funds for security is difficult.

According to the Gallup poll, "Did you, yourself, happen to attend church, synagogue or mosque in the last seven days, or not?" It was as high as 49% in the mid 1950's, but has been in the mid-30% range in recent years.

In one study, the actual rate of church attendance from head counts is less than half of the 40 percent the pollsters report. Numbers from actual counts of people in Orthodox Christian churches (Catholic, mainline and evangelical) show that in 2004, 17.7 percent of the population attended a Christian church on any given weekend.

The church attendance decline does not appear to affect evangelical churches. It also does not appear to affect Mormon temples. Currently, 1.9% of the public identifies as Mormon, a number identical to findings from a 2011 study of Mormons in the U.S.

More than 2 in 5 churches[90] (44 percent) only have one or fewer full-time staff members. Close to 9 in 10 pastors (87 percent) say their church had the same or fewer number of full-time staff in 2018 as they had in 2017, including 7 percent who cut staff.

On relative incomes and church membership, PRRI reports as follows: Religious groups with the lowest levels of household incomes tend to be Christians from racial and ethnic minority groups. More than four in ten black Protestants (43%), Hispanic Protestants (45%), Jehovah's Witnesses (45%), and Hispanic Catholics (49%) report household earnings of less than $30,000 per year.

White Christian groups report higher levels of income. Less than one-third of white, evangelical Protestants (28%), Mormons (26%), white, mainline Protestants (22%), and white Catholics (19%) have household incomes of less than $30,000 per year.

Among non-Christian groups, Muslims report the lowest levels of household income. Nearly four in ten (38%) Muslims have household incomes of less than $30,000 per year, compared to less than one-third of Buddhists (31%), Hindus (20%), and Jews (16%). One-quarter (25%) of Hindus and 30% of Jewish Americans have annual household incomes in excess of $100,000. Unitarians-Universalists are also fairly well off financially. Only 18% report living in households making less than $30,000 annually, and 22% report having incomes exceeding $100,000.

Many black Christian churches of all affiliated and non-affiliated denominations tend to have lower family incomes than their white counterparts.

When one combines declining church memberships across all faiths (with some exceptions already noted) and an ethnic shift in certain churches (especially Catholic) that also correlates with lower incomes plus some groups such as Moslems and black families with low household incomes, the impact on religious institutions is less operating revenue, reduced staffing and less security support and improvements.

Exactly at the time of the shift in the ethnic character of American churches and declining household incomes of those attending church, synagogue, mosque or temple there is a rising negative security profile brought about by a perfect storm of threats, including terrorism, antisemitism, white supremacism, racism (against blacks and Muslims), hostility from pro- and anti-abortion groups, gender issues, sexual abuse of congregants (reported mainly in the Catholic church) and domestic strife including people who are mentally ill. Overall, there is a rise in hate crimes of all kinds, enough to create deep concern in many jurisdictions.

Faced with all this, churches, synagogues, temples and mosques face a financial crunch along with a certain amount of congregational resistance to the presence of security in the form of guards and surveillance on church property.

A good indicator is what happened at the Poway Chabad Synagogue where an active shooter was able to walk into the house of worship unimpeded because, as the rabbi there explained, the synagogue had no money to pay for guards.

Outside Source of Funds

For the most part private outside funding for security from foundations is limited. Many municipalities and states are offering grant support, but overall the amount of money available isn't enough to satisfy overall needs.

The most robust financial support program in the United States is through FEMA.

FEMA runs a Nonprofit Security Grant Program (NSGP) that is a major source of funds for religious organizations. Funding for 2019 is set at $60 million as it was in 2018. Before 2018 the annual amount available from FEMA was $25 million. The significant increase in funds represents both the growth in demand for assistance and the increase in hate-related crimes in the United States.

IMPORTANT NOTE: If you are going to apply for NSGP and have not obtained a Data Universal Numbering System (DUNS) number and/or are not currently registered in the System for Award Management (SAM), please take immediate action to obtain a DUNS Number, if applicable, and then register immediately in SAM. It may take four weeks or more after you submit your SAM registration before your registration is active in SAM, then an additional 24 hours for Grants.gov to recognize your information. Information on obtaining a DUNS number and registering in SAM is available from Grants.gov.[91]

Of the $60 million allocated for NSGP, $50 million is reserved for designated urban areas. Non-designated urban area grants are identified as NSGP-S. Urban area grants are designated as NSGP-UA.

In Fiscal year (FY) 2018, the Nonprofit Security Grant Program (NSGP) expanded, for the first time to include allowable costs for security training for all nonprofit staff, security planning related costs, and exercises related costs, in addition to the traditionally allowable equipment.

In FY 2019, Nonprofits are encouraged to apply for additional costs, including contracted security personnel as well as security-related training for:

- Employed or volunteer security staff to attend security-related training within the United States;
- Employed or volunteer security staff to attend security-related training within the United States with the intent of training other staff or members/congregants upon completing the training (i.e., "train-the-trainer" type courses);
- Employed or volunteer security staff or members/congregants to receive on-site security training.
- NOTE: In previous years, one bonus point for any application was added by FEMA to the score for nonprofit organizations that had never received NSGP funding. In FY 2019 and beyond, ten bonus points will be added to the score of applicants.

FEMA has also produced for 2019 a Preparedness Grant Manual[92] which guides applicants through the process.

NSGP-UA Eligible Areas

- Arizona: Phoenix Area
- California: Anaheim/Santa Ana Area; Bay Area; Los Angeles/Long Beach Area; Riverside Area; Sacramento Area; San Diego Area
- Colorado: Denver Area
- District of Columbia: National Capital Region
- Florida: Miami/Fort Lauderdale Area; Orlando, Tampa Area
- Georgia: Atlanta Area
- Hawaii: Honolulu Area. Illinois: Chicago Area
- Maryland: Baltimore Area
- Massachusetts: Boston Area
- Michigan: Detroit Area
- Minnesota: Twin Cities Area
- Missouri: St. Louis Area
- Nevada: Las Vegas Area
- New Jersey: Jersey City/Newark Area
- New York: New York City Area
- North Carolina: Charlotte Area
- Oregon: Portland Area
- Pennsylvania: Philadelphia Area; Pittsburgh Area
- Texas: Dallas/Fort Worth/Arlington Area; Houston Area: San Antonio Area
- Virginia: Hampton Roads Area
- Washington: Seattle

NSGP-S Target Allocations

Take note that the list below is presented in the order presented by FEMA. No explanation is provided for the amounts allocated to states and territories of the United States.

- Alabama $200,000
- Montana $100,000
- Alaska $100,000
- Nebraska $150,000

- American Samoa $100,000
- Nevada $100,000
- Arizona $150,000
- New Hampshire $150,000
- Arkansas $200,000
- New Jersey $150,000
- California $300,000
- New Mexico $150,000
- Colorado $150,000
- New York $300,000
- Connecticut $200,000
- North Carolina $300,000 –
- Delaware $100,000
- North Dakota $100,000 –
- District of Columbia N/A
- Northern Mariana Islands $100,000
- Florida $250,000
- Ohio $400,000
- Georgia $250,000
- Oklahoma $200,000
- Guam $100,000
- Oregon $150,000
- Hawaii $100,000
- Pennsylvania $250,000
- Idaho $150,000
- Puerto Rico $200,000
- Illinois $250,000
- Rhode Island $100,000
- Indiana $250,000
- South Carolina $200,000
- Iowa $200,000
- South Dakota $100,000
- Kansas $150,000

- Tennessee $250,000
- Kentucky $200,000
- Texas $400,000
- Louisiana $200,000
- U.S. Virgin Islands $100,000
- Maine $150,000
- Utah $150,000
- Maryland $150,000
- Vermont $100,000
- Massachusetts $250,000
- Virginia $200,000
- Michigan $250,000
- Washington $200,000
- Minnesota $150,000
- West Virginia $150,000
- Mississippi $150,000
- Wisconsin $250,000
- Missouri $200,000
- Wyoming $100,000

As should be clear, the funds for nonprofit organizations in states and localities outside of designated urban areas is quite limited.

The FY 2019 NSGP supports investments that improve the ability of organizations nationwide to:

- Prevent a threatened or an actual act of terrorism;
- Protect our citizens, residents, visitors, and assets against the greatest threats and hazards;
- Mitigate the loss of life and property by lessening the impact of future disasters;
- Respond quickly to save lives, protect property and the environment, and meet basic human needs in the aftermath of a catastrophic incident; and/or

- Recover through a focus on the timely restoration, strengthening, and revitalization of infrastructure, housing, and a sustainable economy, as well as the health, social, cultural, historic, and environmental fabric of communities affected by a catastrophic incident.

The NSGP provides funding support for hardening and other physical security enhancements to nonprofit organizations that are at high risk of terrorist attack.

The program seeks to integrate the preparedness activities of nonprofit organizations that are at high risk of terrorist attack with broader state, local, tribal and territorial (SLTT) preparedness efforts.

FEMA individual grants are generally capped at $100,000 per year, although exceptions may be made.

Applications are through State Administrative Agencies unless covered under Urban Area Grants.

ONLINE INFORMATION: The Notice of Funding Opportunity (NOFO) is the official document that contains all information and requirements for the FY 2019 NSGP. The FY 2019 NSGP NOFO is located online (at http://www.fema.gov/grants as well as on www.grants.gov.) Future year NOFO information should be checked at the locations listed.

An eligible nonprofit organization must:
- Meet the description under section 501(c)(3) of the Internal Revenue Code of 1986 (IRC) and exempt from tax under section 501(a) of such code;
- For NSGP-UA, be located within one of the FY 2019 UASI[93]-designated urban areas; OR for NSGP-S, be located outside of the FY 2019 UASI-designated urban areas; and

- Be able to demonstrate, through the application, that the organization is at high risk of a terrorist attack.

Ways an organization can substantiate that it is at high risk of a terrorist attack include:

- Describe any incidents that have occurred at the facility.
- Describe any threats (e.g. verbal threats, vandalism) made against the organization.
- Monitor current events with specific attention to incidents impacting organizations that have been targeted due to a similar mission, belief, or ideology.

Contact organizations/agencies that can provide information on the current threat environment such as local law enforcement offices, local emergency management offices, Federal Bureau of Investigation Field offices, or Regional Protective Security Advisors. To reach a Protective Security Advisor, email NICC@hq.dhs.gov.

The following are some of the allowable costs that can be covered by a FEMA Grant:

- Planning – Activities related to the development of plans such as
- Security Risk Management Plans
- Continuity of Operations Plans
- Response Plans
- Equipment – Authorized Equipment including
- Access control equipment
- Surveillance equipment
- Physical protective measures such as concrete barriers
- Training
- Active Shooter Training
- Security Training for employees, or members/congregation
- Exercises
- Response exercise

Each eligible nonprofit organization must submit the following to their SAA:

- Vulnerability/Risk Assessment

A vulnerability/risk assessment specific to the location/facility for which the nonprofit organization is applying. Currently, there are no other FEMA specific requirements for the vulnerability assessment.

For a list of authorized equipment, please check here FEMA's authorized-equipment-list available online.

NSGP Investment Justification (IJ)

The IJ is the application form used to apply for NSGP. It must include the nonprofit organization's risks, vulnerabilities, and the proposed projects that are intended to address/mitigate the identified risks and vulnerabilities. Proposed projects must be for the locations that the nonprofit occupies at the time of application. Applicants can find the NSGP IJ DHS/FEMA Form 089-24 (OMB Control Number: 1660-0110) on grants.gov (Search Grants Tab; CDFA: 97.008).

Mission Statement

A Mission Statement [what the organization does, such as provide religious instruction, prayer groups etc.] and any mission implementing policies or practices that may elevate the organization's risk must be submitted. DHS will use the Mission Statement along with the information provided in the IJ to determine the central purpose of the organization and will validate the FY 2019 NSGP FAQs for Nonprofit Organizations

Nonprofits 'organization type' selected by the nonprofit organization on the IJ.

The organization type may be one of the following:

- Ideology based/Spiritual/Religious;
- Educational;
- Medical; or
- Other (Not Defined)

Supporting documentation related to actual incidents that have occurred at the location/facility, if applicable. If applicable, nonprofit organizations may include any proof of actual incidents that have occurred at the location or facility; this includes items such as police reports or photographs.

What makes a strong IJ?

- Clearly identified risks, vulnerabilities, and consequences;
- Description of findings from a previously conducted vulnerability assessment;
- Details of any incident(s) including description, dates etc.;
- A brief description of any supporting documentation (such as police reports or photographs) that is submitted as part of the application, if applicable;
- Explanation of how the investments proposed will mitigate or address the vulnerabilities identified from a vulnerability assessment;
- Establish a clear linkage with investment(s) and core capabilities (See National Preparedness Goal); see http://www.fema.gov/national-preparedness-goal for information on core capabilities
- Verify all proposed activities are allowable costs per the FY 2019 NSGP NOFO;
- Realistic milestones that considers the Environmental Planning and Historic Preservation (EHP) review process, if applicable; and
- Description of the project manager(s) level of experience.

An organization may apply for multiple locations of the same organization, but for each location/facility that you apply for, you must:

- Submit a complete Investment Justification;
- Have a vulnerability assessment specific to the location/facility that you are applying for; and
- Ensure that the total amount you are requesting for all locations/facilities does not exceed $100,000

Author's Observation on US Nonprofit Funding Levels

The US program, which has been increased to an overall level of $60 million annually is still far from adequate.

The FEMA program is funded out of FEMA funding allocations and the faith- based initiative is not separately legislated. New legislative proposals have recently been introduced to establish the grant program and fund it separately.

The amount of funds available both to put in place security systems and hire guards and the need to maintain and support these systems and personnel falls below what is actually needed.

In the author's opinion, a properly funded program would run at a minimum of $250 million annually. I have proposed that the US government provide $1 billion annually for the protection of holy places[94]. This may sound like a lot, but actually it is a modest investment on a nationwide basis. What I said a few years ago still holds: "Today, it is reported that the United States has spent more than $5.6 trillion[95] on Iraq, Afghanistan and Syria fighting terrorism. Going forward, as ISIS is almost defeated, but its terrorist activities are rapidly spreading in our direction, better protection of our faith-based institutions is a national security necessity. That means we have to make the resources available, including a significant increase in funding for vital security grants."

At present, without legislation, there is not much chance for any dramatic further increase in FEMA money. Moreover, state and local grants (outside of FEMA money), such as they are, generally are very small when compared to need. Proposed legislative remedies (such as by Senator Rob Portman and Congressman Gary Peters) provide a very modest funding increase and no funding increase for urban areas. Separately, U.S. Senators Martha McSally (R-Ariz.) and Martin Heinrich (D-N.M.) introduced legislation to ensure that the Department of Homeland Security (DHS) provide state and local law enforcement with adequate resources to protect faith-based community centers and houses of worship across the United States.

The bill includes $75 million in additional funding to DHS under the existing State Homeland Security Grant Program, bringing the total program to $135 million. McSally and Heinrich and with 31 bipartisan colleagues also asked the Chairman of the Senate Appropriations Committee to add the $75 million to current Department of Homeland Security funding.

It may take some time to complete the legislative process in both houses of Congress. Also note that authorization legislation does not assure funding: that requires separate appropriations legislation. All of this means that outside of a national emergency, moving new legislation successfully through the Congress can take some time.

Canadian Matching Grant Program

Canada provides matching funds for nonprofit organizations at risk. The Canadian program is a good deal smaller than the US. Public Safety Canada has spent more than C$7-million (Canadian dollars) since 2012 upgrading security at religious institutions through its Security Infrastructure Program[96].

Approved projects may receive up to 50% of total project costs to a maximum Public Safety Canada contribution of C$100,000 per project. Funding is available to not-for-profit organizations that are at risk of being victimized by hate-motivated crime. It helps with the costs of security infrastructure improvements for places of worship provincially and territorially recognized private educational institutions, and community centers. Certain costs are not covered by the Canadian program and applicants should get the latest update on restrictions. For example, Guard services are not funded under the Security Infrastructure Program.

Applicants are now encouraged to submit their completed application (including their budget, their quotes and other supporting documents) using an online application form[97].

To help applicants and contractors, Public Safety Canada has also created a Standardized Quote Template and Quote Sample and a Security Equipment Pricing Guide[98]. The guide is a list of the most popular equipment and their fair market value. The guide will be used to assess funding applications.

To be eligible for funding, a minimum of two (2) comparable quotes on each equipment items need to be included with your application using the Standardized Quote Template.

Canadian Funding criteria

Approved projects may receive up to 50% of total project costs to a maximum Public Safety Canada contribution of C$100,000 per project.

Proposals may be approved in their entirety or in part.

IMPORTANT: Applicants must demonstrate that they are able to provide at least 50% of the total project costs. These contributions must be from non-governmental sources and must be available at the time the application is submitted.

Funding or reimbursements cannot be provided to applicants for any activities that have been started or completed prior to signing a contribution agreement with Public Safety Canada.

Funding is available to not-for-profit organizations that are at risk of being victimized by hate-motivated crime. It helps with the costs of security infrastructure improvements for places of worship, provincially and territorially recognized private educational institutions, and community centers.

Crown Corporations, publicly funded institutions, for-profit organizations and individuals are not eligible for funding.

There is an Application Guide[99] available.

Funding is available to three types of not-for-profit organizations that are at risk of being victimized by hate-motivated crime:

Places of worship such as a temple, mosque, synagogue, gurdwara or church, where a group of people can gather to perform acts of religious praise, meditation, honor or devotion;

Provincially/territorially recognized private educational institutions, including primary and secondary schools; and

Community centers, such as a community drop-in center or aboriginal Friendship Center, where members of a community can gather year-round for social or cultural activities.

Canada–Eligible costs
- Security assessments (report and consultation fees) not to exceed 25% of total project cost. Please note that security assessments conducted prior to signing a contribution agreement with Public Safety Canada will not be eligible for reimbursement. Applicants who have received a Crime Prevention through Environmental Design (CPTED) assessment from a police service will not be eligible for reimbursement for any subsequent security assessments;
- Minor construction related to the project (contractor fees, labor, equipment rental, installation fees)
- Security equipment and hardware costs, including alarm systems, fences, gates, locks, security access systems, lighting, security film for windows, relocation of existing cameras, anti-graffiti sealant, motion detectors, signage and landscaping consistent with a CPTED assessment;
- Closed circuit television systems (CCTV) which may include interior and exterior cameras, digital video recorder, monitor, and installation costs associated with the system including wiring, brackets and accessories. The system accessories cannot exceed 25% of the total cost of the CCTV system;
- Training costs for proper use of new security equipment; and
- Project related monitoring, reporting and evaluation costs.

Canada–Ineligible costs
- Capital costs that include land, construction or renovation of buildings, and vehicles;
- Salaries and wages for full-time personnel;
- Hospitality and travel;

- Core or ongoing operating expenses related to the project, including maintenance
- Equipment and/or hardware which includes any of the following: benches, concrete barrier wall, doors, emergency automated telephone system, walkie talkies, fingerprint reader system, heat sensors, night vision goggles, body armor, panic button, projectors, reflector mirrors, security desk, smoke alarms, radios, intercom or public address systems, hidden cameras or dummy cameras, windows, window bars and tire shredders and any other equipment or hardware not related to deterring hate motivated crime; and
- Hiring of security guards.

In Canada, project proposals are reviewed against the following criteria:
- The demonstration and frequency of hate-motivated incidents against the project site;
- The demonstration of how the applicant's community is at risk of being targeted by hate-motivated crime;
- The security infrastructure equipment currently in place;
- The ability of the applicant to develop, implement, manage, monitor, and document a project within a specified timeframe and budget.

Canada Reporting Requirement

Successful applicants will be required to submit a final project report to Public Safety Canada three months after project completion. A Project Officer will provide you with a template which will capture the following:
- A complete description of funded security infrastructure upgrades;
- The extent to which the work plan for the project was implemented;
- Lessons learned as a result of implementing the project;
- The impact of the project at the project site, (e.g. the extent to which the organization experienced a decrease in the number of hate-motivated crimes as a result of security infrastructure upgrades); and

- The extent to which funding recipients report an increased sense of security after project completion as a result of security infrastructure upgrades.

UK Government Grants

In the UK, government support is relatively small.

The amount available for religious buildings seeking to enhance premises will rise to £1.6 million ($2.06 million) in 2019-20.

Launched in 2016, the Places of Worship Security Fund helps churches, mosques, temples and gurdwaras in England and Wales to install alarms, security lighting, fencing and CCTV cameras to deter attackers.

The scheme is one of the main commitments contained within the Government Hate Crime Action Plan[100]. It will provide funding for protective security measures to places of worship that are vulnerable to hate crime.

Places of worship can submit bids for projects costing up to £70,000 for protective security measures and will be required to contribute at least 20 percent of the total cost of the project. The Home Office will award funding on a discretionary basis up to a maximum of £56,000 per place of worship.

Funding will not be available for improvements, lead theft, security upgrades or measures to tackle anti-social behavior or other criminality unconnected with hate crime.

Examples of places of worship eligible to apply for the funding, but this is not an exhaustive list:

- Churches
- Gurdwaras (places of worship for Sikhs)
- Mosques
- Temples

Faith schools, educational institutions, community centers, NHS establishments [National Health Service] (including chapels and prayer rooms) are not eligible to apply.

If a vicarage, manse, community or church hall is attached to the place of worship building, only the building used for worship is eligible for funding.

The Jewish community are not eligible for funding from this scheme as a similar commitment was made to fund Jewish community sites through a grant administered by the Community Security Trust[101] (CST).

The CST provides security advice and training for Jewish schools, synagogues and communal organizations and gives assistance to those bodies that are affected by antisemitism. Antisemitism in the UK has greatly increased in the past few years.

The CST assists and supports individual members of the Jewish community who have been affected by antisemitism and antisemitic incidents. It advises and represents the Jewish community on matters of antisemitism, terrorism and security and works with police, government and international bodies. All this work is provided at no charge.

The UK Home Office has provided Jewish Community Protective Security Grant funding for the security of synagogues, schools and other Jewish centers, with the CST as the Grant Recipient. It was introduced in 2015 and *Home Secretary*, Sajid Javid has pledged to increase funding bringing the amount allocated since its introduction to £65.2 million ($84.1 million).

The Jewish Community Protective Security Grant, like other Home Office Grants, is awarded annually.

Under the Grant educational sites are a priority and all registered schools, colleges and nurseries are offered funding for security.

The Home Office works with the Security Community Trust throughout each year to consider how the Grant is being operated and what is being delivered across all areas.

In 2019, the UK government allocated £14 million ($18.0 million) for the security of synagogues, schools and other Jewish centers—up from £13.4 million ($17.9 million) in 2018.

More than a hundred antisemitic incidents a month were reported to the CST, producing a total of 1,652 for 2018.

According to Victoria Atkins, the Parliamentary under Secretary of State for the Home Department, The Jewish Community Protective Security Grant was introduced in 2015 following a series of terrorist attacks against Jews and

Jewish locations across Europe and the West, including Paris, Copenhagen, Brussels and Marseilles.

International terrorist propaganda, particularly by ISIS has repeatedly highlighted Jews as targets for terrorist attacks. The grant mainly funds security guarding at Jewish schools, nurseries and some synagogues

The Places of Worship Protective Security Funding Scheme is specifically for the provision of protective security measures such as access control, fencing and lighting for places of worship that are vulnerable to hate crime attacks.

The Home Secretary announced a boost in funding for the hate crime Places of Worship Protective Security Funding Scheme to £1.6 million for 2019/20. This is double the amount awarded in 2018/19. In addition, £5 million over three years has been committed to providing security training to places of worship in England and Wales.

The Jewish Community Protective Security Grant makes funding available to all Jewish free, state and independent schools, colleges and nurseries to employ security guards during operating hours, and to improve security at many synagogues and other communal locations through the implementation of guarding and physical security measures. These funded security measures supplement existing site security arrangements and policing measures.

Applications are handled through CST.

In addition, as a Charitable Trust, CST runs its own programs and receives financial support in the form of donations from the community.

CST's Security Enhancement Project funds security facilities, such as CCTV systems, fencing, anti-shatter window film, locks and alarms, at hundreds of Jewish buildings across the country.

The project's goal is for all Jewish communal premises to meet the recommendations of Government counterterrorism guidance:

- Deter a would-be intruder, by providing physical and electronic security measures, coupled with good management practices.
- Detect an intrusion, by providing alarm and visual-detection systems with verification.

- Delay an intrusion for a sufficient period of time to allow a response force to attend, by putting in place the appropriate, physical security measures.

Australia

Australia has announced it is expanding its Safer Communities Fund, which will now include religious schools, places of worship and places of religious assembly.

The Safer Communities Fund makes grants available from A-$50,000 ($34,496) to A-$1.5 million ($1.03 million) to implement safety enhancements including CCTV, lighting, fencing, bollards, alarms, security systems and public address systems.

A report[102] released in 2018 by the Executive Council of Australian Jewry found a 60 per cent rise in antisemitic incidents across Australia in 2018, citing 156 attacks on Jewish community groups, including synagogues and Jewish schools that amounted to assault, abuse, vandalism and graffiti.

Australia's Prime Minister announced that grants would be available up to A-$55 million ($38 million).

The Safer Communities Fund provides grants of up to $1 million to community organizations and local governments for local crime prevention and security infrastructure activities and to protect community organizations that may be facing security risks associated with racial and /or religious intolerance. Project activities can include:

- Installation of fixed or mobile CCTV cameras
- Installation of security lighting
- Installation of bollards
- Installation of security and alarm systems, intercoms and swipe access attached to a public or community space
- Crime prevention through environmental design (CPTED) including changing environmental characteristics in public or community spaces, such as a lack of lighting or poor natural surveillance that can facilitate street crime and violence.

- Grants of up to A-$1 million ($690,000) are available to fund up to 100 per cent of eligible project costs.
- Projects must be completed by 31 March 2020.

To be eligible, you must:

- Have an Australian Business Number (ABN) and be one of the following entities: an incorporated, not-for-profit organization or local government agencies or bodies, industry/trader associations and chambers of commerce can apply if they meet the eligibility criteria above.

In order to be eligible, you must:

- Provide evidence from the site owner or manager providing authority for you to undertake the project at the nominated site. You should use the letter template provided for the grant and provide this with your application or prior to entering into a grant agreement.
- Be able to start your project within 8 weeks of executing a grant agreement which can include project planning activities.
- Have met relevant state or territory legislation obligations related to working with children, and ensure that any person that has direct, unsupervised contact with children as part of a project under this program, has undertaken and passed a Working with Children check, if required under relevant State or Territory legislation. You are also responsible for assessing the suitability of the people you engage as part of your project to ensure children are kept safe.

You are not eligible to apply if you are:

- A school or preschool that is registered as an educational establishment with a state or territory registration authority.[103]

Jewish Agency Funding

Israel provides funds for synagogue and Jewish school security worldwide through the Jewish Agency.

According to the Jewish Agency[104]: "Although the majority of the world's Jews today live in physical safety, there are still significant numbers of Jews around the globe living in unaccepting locations, among antisemitic populations."

"Security details are needed for Jewish centers and activities in communities including Argentina, Greece, Brazil, and South Africa. The Jewish Agency for Israel assists these communities in implementing special security measures at schools, Jewish community centers, and synagogues." An Emergency Assistance Fund ensures that communities can upgrade security, such as video surveillance & CCTV, alarms, locks, gates, and reinforced walls/doors/windows.

Things to Keep in Mind

Available Grants to help pay the cost of holy places security is gaining more and more public attention and governments, including federal, state and local (counties, cities and towns, townships, various jurisdictions) are stepping up their efforts. While private grants from philanthropies are far behind, they will catch up in time. It is important to keep in mind that this space is changing and greater efforts in the future can be expected.

But the issue of paying for security is still a challenge for congregations, and will remain so for those with smaller congregations and more precarious budgets.

Some congregations are starting to realize they need to charge separately for security services such as guards and they also need volunteers from their congregation to perform security-related tasks. Almost all of them need better training.

The good news is that the US government now recognizes that its funding has to go beyond infrastructure and include money for guards and for training. But even with the additional money "in the Federal pot," even when supplemented by state and local grants, is not enough to get the job done.

Furthermore, the existing US program has a fundamental flaw. If you are a congregation that was not directly threatened, you have no case to make to request Federal support or at least that is the import of the guidelines currently circulated.

Yet we know that domestic and international threats generally look for unprotected or poorly, safeguarded religious organizations as an opportunity for violence.

Worse still, none of the programs recognize that up to half the incidents come about from domestic conflict and mental illness.

This leaves all religious organizations, especially underfunded ones, in a significant quandary, and that is multiplied if they otherwise do not qualify because they have not encountered any domestic threat aimed at them specifically.

The experience of the Sutherland Springs First Baptist Church is a case in point –in fact, there is more than one point to make.

The first is that Sutherland Springs First Baptist Church never expected an active shooter incident or that so many in its congregation would be killed or wounded.

Sutherland Spring would not have qualified for a FEMA grant for security. In fact, it had absolutely no security, whether by choice or not we don't know.

In some ways the outcome after the shooting is also concerning.

The old Sutherland Spring church, where the killing and wounding happened, has been turned into a memorial for those who died.

That building is no longer an active church. It has been replaced by a $3 million new church paid for by the North American Mission Board. The new church is located on the same lot, a few feet away from the old church.

The new church's security team now practices active shooter training in the church. They learned how to use flashlights to disarm attackers and developed defense tactics based on the shape and structure of the new building.

The team, made up of volunteer congregants, was formed after the mass shooting.

In addition to the security team, the new building was designed to prevent another shooting, with security features such as additional cameras and keyed access.

These are good steps, but where are the armed guards? Can the church, now the tallest building in a 600-person community, find ways to keep it safe in the years ahead?

There are no good answers, especially when a church acquires an expensive new plant that has to be supported and maintained.

Another issue to be considered: Sutherland Springs First Baptist Church is not in an urban area and therefore has to compete for FEMA grant money across the entire state, where the allocation from FEMA is way too small to accommodate more than a few congregations.

Hate crimes in particular can happen in rural areas as often as in urban ones. The differentiation put into effect by FEMA may be in need of reconsideration, or more like, the amount of funding for non-urban areas must be increased.

TAKE NOTE: Grant amounts and Grant instructions are subject to change. Please refer to the latest updated grant application information for the relevant country program.

Voluntary and Less than Voluntary Monetary Contributions

Some holy places are adding a security fee to the dues of their congregants, or asking for a specific cash contribution for security on a voluntary basis.

This is a good step, but not enough in many cases where the congregation is poor or small, and not all congregations will go along with additional fees and charges.

Over time each religious organization (and this implies all houses of worship, religious schools and community centers) will have to reach its own conclusion on what to do, and see if it can find money for security, either from assessed contributions of all members, or by grants from individual congregants or foundations willing to support them.

Security fees vary a lot and there is as yet no standard practice. Some charge a mandatory fee—one amount required for individual memberships and another for family memberships. Others have a flat fee that is associated with the membership fee.

If there is no membership fee, the congregation may have to rely on voluntary contributions. This is more difficult, as getting congregants to pay on a voluntary basis may tax even the most exhortative pastor.

In figuring out the best approach, it is important to differentiate between capital costs and operational ones. Capital costs refer mainly to acquisition and maintenance of security equipment, which is usually based on the Security Plan or the discovery of some new vulnerability. Capital costs can be subdivided into regular needs and emergency requirements. Regular needs may include a camera system or an alarm system. An emergency need may occur if there was some incident that has revealed a major infrastructure weakness, for example, poor door locks or the need for a fireproof roof.

Operational costs include the need to have a security company support daily operations (protection against burglars, vandalism, fires) or to pay guards. Also included is the need to keep equipment and infrastructure in good repair.

Training may also require hiring security companies or specialists to help train staff, volunteers and the congregation.

In addition, the inventory of supplies (bandages, stretchers, medical supplies, etc.) need to be checked and updated.

The system also needs constant testing.

There is an unfortunate tendency to buy equipment and then not keep it up or exercise it, or to keep continuity by making sure staff, including transitioning and new staff, understand what is needed to keep security systems viable and operational.

There are even cases where equipment is acquired under a grant and then left in the shipment boxes and never used.

All these things impact the budget and keeping up the new overhead is an important consideration going forward.

A good case study was provided by the Jewish Telegraphic Agency[105]. In one case in New York in a synagogue they found that the overall cost for security systems was around $150,000. That number did not include some of the window and camera costs, which [the rabbi] paid for partly out of a $50,000 grant from New York state. And the armed guards, contracted from a private security company at $40 an hour each, cost about $360 per week.

There are few houses of worship that can get away from spending at least $50,000 to $100,000 on security infrastructure and probably a lot more, depending on the security challenges, the size of the structure and its campus, and the perception of threat. And none of this includes continuing costs to maintain the security apparatus.

All of this means real pressure on budgets and the need for additional funding, much of it coming from the congregation.

CHAPTER 10

Security Committees

Religious organizations with, or without large staffs should establish a Security Committee.

A Security Committee often is made up of congregants who volunteer, and sometimes the volunteers are either augmented by paid staff or work with paid staff.

For an effective Security Committee to operate it needs to be authorized and backed by the Board of Directors or other governing authority in the church organization. It also must have the support of the religious leadership, since many choices that the Committee will need to make can have religious and moral implications in which the church leader will want to be consulted.

There are many lay resources to draw upon in congregations, including active and retired police and military, security experts, physicians, people with exceptional technical knowledge and attorneys who can help assist in contracting with guards and helping assure that the Security Committee is not legally liable.

A Security Committee can, with professional assistance, carry out a vulnerability analysis, formulate a Security Plan, and assist in making sure that the infrastructure and guards, as well as security volunteers can work harmoniously and productively.

A Security Committee may also integrate safety considerations into its work.

I have adapted BWX Technologies[106] Security and Safety Committee Charter as a good guide for establishing a Security Committee. This Guide can be adapted to suit congregational needs and to apply in different jurisdictions. Its presentation here is not intended to foreclose other formulations that may be proposed.

Security Committee Authority and Responsibilities

The Committee shall:

Appoint a board Chairperson and Deputy Chairperson with the mandate to call periodic Security Board meetings and sign off on completed reports and proposals agreed to by the Security Committee

Receive and review reports of the holy place key safety and security performance indicators and trends, as well as any significant incidents or events including the adequacy of corrective actions

Arrange briefings for the religious place leadership, staff and (where advisable) to the congregants on known threats to the congregation or to the religious community broadly

Review the results of major inspections and propose remedies if the inspections found major issues affecting safety and security, focusing on exterior and interior gaps in coverage

Review any special projects assigned by the organization's Board of Directors, such as installation of cameras, security locks, burglar alarms etc.

Periodically review strategies designed to prevent or address catastrophic operational interruption such as active shooters, fire bombs and other bomb attacks and other emerging security threats

Make sure the facility is in compliance with relevant health and safety laws and regulations

Have the authority to engage outside experts or consultants (including independent or outside counsel), in each case, of its choice and as it determines to be necessary or appropriate in connection with the duties and responsibilities of the Committee, provided the Committee has Board of Directors approval

Form and delegate authority to subcommittees when appropriate make regular reports to the Board of Directors or other supervising authority

Propose budgets needed for all security and safety activities, propose acquisitions of equipment, guard services and other actions required to enhance security and safety

Maintain confidentiality of all security information in the hands of the Committee

Assist in training staff and congregants in security measures

Maintain liaison with local law enforcement, FBI, fire brigades and First Responders

Assist in organizing security drills

Provide guidance to the congregation and seek advice on various safety and security topics

Take such other actions and undertake such other activities as may be referred to it from time to time by the Board

---

The author is grateful to BWX Technologies for their thoughtful presentation.

CHAPTER 11

Conclusions

The idea behind a good security system is to deter an assailant.

There is no perfect way to do this of course, since someone with mental health problems or an insider threat may be impossible to dissuade from launching an attack on a holy place.

Even so, deterrence is quite important and should be looked on as a key component of all security plans.

The most important element for successful deterrence is **security visibility**.

If there is an armed guard that can be seen from outside, or a parked police cruiser, it is less likely that a terrorist (of any description) is going to attack.

Similarly, if there is strong lighting around a church, synagogue, mosque or temple building, it is less likely anyone will take the chance of launching an attack.

Take note that camera systems can be linked to alarm companies and operate full-time (24x7). Also note that saved images from cameras can help identify a malefactor or threat, or even uncover a license plate [number plate].

It is important to stress that most attacks don't just come out of the blue. Terrorists and haters usually plan the attack beforehand, carry out surveillance and even might attend religious services in order to assess the layout of the premises and understand where guards, cameras and alarms are located.

There have been many reports of people in cars photographing churches, synagogues, mosques and temples. Those pictures are used as part of attack planning. Usually the photos will be made during hours of activity (services, meetings, celebrations) so that an active shooter can see how security is organized and what might possibly stop his or her attack.

Similarly, unknown people walking around a religious property are doing the same thing as those doing surveillance in cars, and they may be taking pictures with mobile phones or cameras.

Visible security will help convince them to abandon their plan. In addition, challenging anyone wandering about, asking for identification and being stern with them is an effective measure. **Doing so is safest when it is done by a professional armed guard.**

STRONGLY RECOMMENDED: It is quite important for armed guards to be dressed in a uniform and they should wear protective vests and Kevlar-type helmets. Volunteers also should wear identifying shirts or jackets.

Volunteers should also wear bright jackets or shirts clearly marked with the word "Security." Volunteers should be equipped with radios, and if on site in evening hours, should carry powerful flashlights.

No doubt should be left that the holy place is actively under guard and proactive measures are in place.

Some religious leaders want guards to be unobtrusive, dressed just as others in the congregation.

There are important reasons why this isn't the best approach.

The first is that unobtrusive guards and volunteers lose their deterrent value if they are unrecognizable.

In addition, unmarked guards and volunteers leave the congregation in doubt that they are protected.

Even more importantly, in any incident or emergency, physically finding the guard in a crowd will be difficult and will cause a delay in response.

There also is the fact that visible guards and security volunteers command respect.

In any incident along with confronting the danger they will try and protect the lives of the congregation by directing them in certain ways, such as a lockdown or an evacuation.

IMPORTANT: A uniform or security jacket helps make the guard or volunteer's authority convincing and effective and helps police recognize security personnel on site.

Beyond guards and volunteers, good practice says that the access system to the holy place should be designed to delay an intruder. This is important because it provides an opportunity for intervention and mitigation without immediately exposing congregants to physical threats. It is also important because it creates a time-space to implement internal security procedures such as lock down and, if needed, evacuation.

In this text we have referred a number of times to making use of the few minutes when a threat is detected and before the threat is neutralized to put into operation a well-executed and planned set of security procedures. This is a major change from the FBI's Run, Hide and Fight idea. A disciplined approach to blocking an intruder (starting with deterrence outside) is the better way to go, and techniques such as "benevolent bottlenecks" help significantly.

At the end of the day, for those who attend a religious service, confidence in the security of the holy place is a key component of spirituality.

ABOUT THE AUTHOR

Stephen Bryen is a leading expert in security strategy and technology. He has held senior positions in the Department of Defense, on Capitol Hill and as the President of a large multinational defense and technology company. He currently is a Vice President for Sussman Corporate Security and serves as a senior fellow at three research institutes, is an author and writes for Asia Times and other publications.

Dr. Bryen did his undergraduate work at Rutgers University, received his M.A. and PhD from Tulane University and did post-doctoral work at Virginia Polytechnic Institute and State University. At Tulane, Bryen was a National Defense Scholar.

Dr. Bryen writes for Asia Times, American Thinker, National Interest and Infocus Magazine and for many other newspapers and magazines. He has published four books on security subjects.

Stephen Bryen is a Senior Fellow of the American Center for Democracy. He also serves as a Senior Fellow for Il Nodo di Gordio (The Gordian Knot), a leading thing tank in Italy, and as a Fellow of the Taiwan Institute for Political, Economic and Social Studies.

Dr. Bryen's expertise and high effectiveness has earned him the highest civilian awards of the U.S. Defense Department on two occasions and established him as a proven government, civic and business leader in Washington D.C. and internationally.

- Morley Safer of the CBS Program 60 Minutes said: "Dr. Bryen was the Pentagon's top cop, the man whose job it was to ensure that sensitive technology would be kept from enemies, potential enemies and questionable allies."

- "Bryen came to private industry after a career in government, but even there he was an innovator and entrepreneur. ... A key part of Bryen's portfolio was managing and shepherding US-allied technological cooperation in pursuit of the common defense." -David Silverberg in Homeland Security Magazine (now HS Today).

He was the founder and first director of the Defense Technology Security Administration and served as a Commissioner on the US-China Security and Economic Review Commission.

In the private sector Dr. Bryen was President of Finmeccanica North America (now Leonardo), a multi-national high technology, defense and security conglomerate.

At the Defense Department he was Deputy Under Secretary of Defense and the Director of the Defense Technology Security administration.

ENDNOTES

1   Brit Gun Maker Tasered by Police After Fleeing Illegal Firearms Factory by Sofie Jackson,(Daily Star) May 8, 2019

2   Top 10 Things Know About Federal Firearms Law by Keith Williams from Law Offices of Keith A. Williams

3   See: wgntv/2019/02/16/victims-identified-in-aurora-shooting-gunman-had-prior-felony-conviction

4   Mental Health entry by Wikipedia

5   Inside Edition by Wikipedia

6   Courts-martial in the United States by Wikipedia

7   Texas Department of Public Safety by Wikipedia

8   Mass_Attacks_in_Public_Spaces-2017.pdf by US Secret Service

9   On GAB, an Extremist Friendly Space (New York Times) October 28, 2018

10   Florida Man Arrested in Threats to Kill Jews, by JTA (Times of Israel) June 16, 2019

11   Cesar Sayoc's Path on Social Media by Kevin Roose (New York Times) October 27, 2018

12   Palestinian Terror Groups: Popular Front for the Liberation of Palestine (Jewish Virtual Library)

13   Osama Bin Laden by Biography.Com, April 16, 2019 (Updated)

14   Manchester Suicide Bombing by Eoghan Macguire, Alexander Smith, Jason Cumming and Alex Johnson (NBC News) May 22, 2017

15   Sensing Peroxide Explosives by Bethany Halford (Chemical Engineering News) October 25, 2010

16   2006 Mumbai Train Bombings, Wikipedia

17   2010 Stockholm Bombings, Wikipedia

18   Times Square Car Bombing Attempt, Wikipedia

19   Manchester Arena Bombing, Wikipedia

20 Canada Day, Wikipedia

21 Tovex by Biafo Industries Limited

22 Holiday Terror attack on Antwerp Synagogue Foiled by Alert Security Guards by Hana Levi Julien (Jewish Press) June 11, 2019

23 Why Run, Hide Fight is Flawed by Mike Wood (Police One) June 15, 2016

24 Catholic Health Care in the United States (Catholic Health Association) January, 2019

25 Private Firm Fills Security Gaps in Germany by John Vandiver (Stars and Stripes) July 29, 2007

26 Police Ballistic Helmets (Hard Head Veterans) May 21, 2018

27 Semi-automatic Pistol, Wikipedia

28 What Are Bump Stocks –Federal Ban Goes into Effect by Jennifer Earl (Fox News) March 26, 2018

29 Las Vegas Shooters Deadly Arsenal Revealed by Abigail Miller and Ashley Collman (Daily Mail) January 20, 2018

30 Customs Agents Make 'Unusual' Seizure Of Nearly 53,000 Chinese Gun Parts by by Sasha Ingber (NPR) July 23, 2019

31 Houston Man is First to be Charged under Bump Stock Ban (New York Times) September 5, 2019

32 Alabama Church Wants its own Police Force by Serena Maxwell (Scroll) April 3, 2017

33 Poway Rabbi Urged Hero Border Patrol Agent To Pray Armed by Aiden Pink (Fast Forward) April 29, 2019

34 Security Guard Training Programs, Classes and Requirements (Study.com) May 20, 2018

35 America's gun-toting guards armed with poor training, little oversight by Shoshana Walter and Ryan Gabrielson (Reveal) December 9, 2014

36 Holiday Terror Attack on Antwerp Synagogues Foiled by Alert Security Guards by Hana Levi Julian (Jewish Press) June 11, 2019

37 Parking Lots Can Be Dangerous Places for Assaults by The Home Security Superstore, undated

38 Police: Deaf woman raped at gunpoint in church parking lot by Koko News 5 (ABC) July 18, 2012

39 Tennessee Church Shooting Suspect Is A Sudanese Bodybuilder by Thomas Phippen (Daily Caller) September 24, 2017

40 Philippines unrest: Who are the Abu Sayyaf group? (BBC News) June 14, 2016

41 New Yorkers are reminded that keeping NYC the safest big city is a shared responsibility (NYPD News via Twitter) October 25, 2018

42 Nice attack: police cars guarding promenade barriers were called away moments before lorry struck by Peter Allen (Evening Standard) July 20, 2016

43 US warns of 'heightened' risk of terror attacks on Christmas markets in Europe as Isil loses grip on Mosul and Raqqa by Raf Sanchez(Telegraph) November 22, 2016

44 Islamic State launches 'unprecedented' wave of suicide bombers to try to defend Mosul by Raf Sanchez (Telegraph) November 5, 2016

45 German authorities 'knew about Christmas market terror plot days before the Berlin lorry attack was carried out by Julian Robinson (Daily Mail) December 20, 2016

46 Blunders that let Berlin Christmas terror suspect go free: He was under surveillance for months, arrested and freed three times, and not deported because of a clerical error by Allan Hall, Martin Robinson, Julian Robinson, Stephanie Linning, Stephen Wright, Lucy Osborne, Tom Kelly, Emine Sinmaz (Daily Mail and others) December 21, 2016

47 Ibid

48 Berlin-terror-attack-christmas-marke-truck-final-moment revealed Germany by Harry Walker (Express) December 20, 2016

49 Ibid

50 Anti-Ram-Barrier Rating Systems by Stone Security Systems, November 2, 2009. PDF available on line.

51 Driver charged with murder in Times Square crash by Ray Sanchez, Ellie Kaufman and Madison Park (CNN) May 20, 207

52 Wedding celebration in San Antonio ends in shooting at Catholic church (AP) March 18, 2019

53 Patron Screening Best Practices Guide by Department of Homeland Security, March 2016 (Available online)

54 Historic churches install metal detectors to prevent terrorism by Sara Dorn (New York Post) March 24, 2018

55 Bucks woman accused of killing fellow church member out of jealousy by Patrick Lester and Riley Yates (Morning Call, Allentown PA) April 2. 2008

56 Burying Our Heads in the Sandbox: Ignoring Security at Summer Camp by Joshua Gleis (Huffington Post) May 31, 2015

57 Who Are Antifa? By Anti-Defamation League of the B'nai Brith

58 PETN: the explosive of choice by Robert McKie (Guardian) October 30. 2010

59 RDX Explosive, by the Encyclopaedia Britannica editors, September 10, 2019

60 Characterization of Three Types of Semtex (H, 1A, and 10) by Stephanie Moore, Michele Schantz and William MacCrehan (Wiley Online Library), September 30, 2010

61 How to Survive a Knife Attack by whito93 (Instructables Outside). Undated, available online

62 Hundreds of sexual abuse cases reported at children's camps across U.S. by CBS News (CBS) December 10, 2018

63 Gunshot Detection with Video Analytics Shortens Response Time When Every Second Counts by Surveillance Secure ™ Available online.

64 Kintronics IP Security Solutions

65 Security Guard Training Programs, Classes and Requirements by Study. com. March 20, 2018. Available online.

66 Security Guard License Requirements by Security Guard-License.org Available online.

67 Off Duty Officers, Inc. at LinkedIn

68 Top 10 Armed Security Jobs by SecurityDegreeHub™ Available online.

69 Security Company Contracts Samples by Upcounsel ™ Available online.

70 Professional Liability Insurance by Upcounsel™ Available online.

71 Peace of Mind Technologies™ Available online.

72 Immediate Security Challenges threatening Front Door Security, Peace of Mind Technologies Available online.

73 Becoming a Physical Security Professional (PSP®) by ASIS, Available

online.

74 Professional Code of Conduct by ASIS. Available online.

75 Board Certification Handbook by ASIS. Available online.

76 Is There a Value to Professional Security Certifications? By Dr. Steve Albrecht (Emerging Issues in Security) April 8, 2019

77 The American Board for Certification in Homeland Security (ABCHS) serves a diverse membership of professionals including active and retired military, law enforcement and security experts, first responders, and others dedicated to the important mission of protecting our nation. The ABCHS is comprised of some of the world's leading professionals who have significant experience in homeland security and emergency response.

78 The Association of Threat Assessment Professionals (ATAP) was founded in 1992 as a non-profit organization comprised of law enforcement, prosecutors, mental health professionals, corporate security experts, probation and parole personnel and others involved in the area of threat and violence risk assessment. The purpose of ATAP is to afford its members a professional and educational environment to exchange ideas and strategies to address such issues as stalking, threats, and homeland security. The primary focus of this organization is to provide the necessary knowledge, tools, and support to better prepare our membership to handle these types of situations. Our commitment is to expertly address these issues through seminars and training and networking with other professionals working in this field.

79 Penn State's online homeland security portfolio is built around a foundational all-hazards approach to homeland security that is applicable to both the public and private sector with options and certificates in a variety of specializations.

80 Global Society of Homeland and National Security Professionals

81 See the Risk-Management page of the Evangelical Lutheran Church in America. It is one of the largest Christian denominations in the United States, with about 4 million members in nearly 10,000 congregations across the United States, Puerto Rico and the U.S. Virgin Islands.

82 Catholic Mutual Group Church Security Guidelines available online.

83 See CMGconnect.org

84 See catholicmutual.org

85 Catholic Mutual Group offers an Emergency Response Procedure (ERP) application for smartphones for parishes, schools, and other religious institutions. This application offers step-by-step directions to guide you through numerous emergency situations from your mobile device. Guidelines on responding to medical emergencies, severe weather, and armed intruders are just a few of the convenient best practices available on this new application. There is also a 'quick-call' feature to contact emergency personnel or applicable contacts during an emergency. Utilizing the ERP application gives clear and practical information in the event of an emergency situation. **Available on APP stores.**

86 Church background checks through Protect My Ministry are designed to help ministries implement and maintain a thorough background screening program for employees, staff and volunteers. Preventing sexual predators and violent offenders from working with children and youth is our primary concern.

87 Best Practices for Mosque and Community Safety by the Council on American-Islamic Relations. Available online.

88 Secure Community Network of the Jewish Federations of North America

89 This organization has trained 4,000 Jewish volunteers to keep synagogues safe by Josafen Dolsten (Jewish Telegraphic Agency) November 6, 2017

90 How Many US Churches are Actually Growing by Aaron Earls (Facts and Trends), March 6, 2019. Since January 1957, *Facts & Trends* has been providing Christian leaders with relevant information, practical ministry ideas, and biblical resource

91 Register at Grants.gov Grants also offers an APP for smartphone for iPhone and Android.

92 FEMA offers Preparedness Grants Manual available online at the FEMA website.

93 Urban Areas Security Initiative (UASI) Program is available on the Homeland Security website.

94 $1 billion for Security Grants for Faith-based Institutions an Urgent Need by Stephen Bryen on my blog page bryensblog.com

95   Cost of U.S. War on Jihadists: $5.6 Trillion, 7,000 Deaths, 52,500 Injuries (Breibart) article based on a study by the Brown University's Watson Institute for International and Public Affairs

96   Communities at Risk: Security Infrastructure Program (SIP) by Public Safety Canada. Available online.

97   The Survey is now closed.

98   Standardized Quote Template and Quote Sample by Public Safety Canada. Available online.

99   Communities at Risk: Security Infrastructure Program Application Guide by Public Safety Canada. Available online.

100   Hate crime action plan 2016 to 2020 by UK Government. Available online.

101   CST is Community Security Trust, a charity that protects British Jews from antisemitism and related threats. CST received charitable status in 1994 and is recognised by the Police and Government as a unique model of best practice. CST has over 90 full and part-time staff based in offices in London, Manchester and Leeds.

102   Report on Antisemitism in Australia 2018 by Julie Nathan, Research Officer (Executive Council of Australian Jewry), October 1, 2017 – September 30, 2018

103   Safer Communities Fund Round 3 - Infrastructure Grants by Business. gov.au

104   Social Action Assistance Fund by the Jewish Agency. Available online.

105   Here's what it costs to put your synagogue under armed by Ben Sales (Jewish Telegraphic Agency), November 13, 2018.

106   BWX Technologies Security and Safety Committee Charter. Available online. BWX Technologies, Inc. (BWXT) is a leading supplier of nuclear components and fuel to the U.S. government; provides technical, management and site services to support governments in the operation of complex facilities and environmental remediation activities; and supplies precision manufactured components, services and CANDU® fuel for the commercial nuclear power industry.

CPSIA information can be obtained
at www.ICGtesting.com
Printed in the USA
JSHW021500300620
6407JS00002B/55